6-20-2018

Dear Sandy,

Thank you for your years of service to this Leadership Team as a member of the Financial Advisory Board!

God bless!
Diane
Barbara
Sharon
Mary

CONGREGATION
FOR INSTITUTES OF CONSECRATED LIFE
AND SOCIETIES OF APOSTOLIC LIFE

ECONOMY
AT THE SERVICE OF CHARISM
AND MISSION

Boni dispensatores multiformis gratiae Dei
(*1 Pt.* 4:10)

GUIDELINES

LIBRERIA EDITRICE VATICANA

Prima edizione Marzo 2018
Prima ristampa Aprile 2018

ISBN 978-88-266-0097-0

*Good stewards responsible
for all these varied graces of God.*

(*1 Pt.* 4:10)

INTRODUCTION

1. *Each one of you has received a special grace, so, like good stewards responsible for all these varied graces of God, put it at the service of others* (*1 Pt.* 4:10).

The *First Letter of Peter* addresses the adversities faced by the Christian communities of the Roman diaspora towards the end of the first century: a moment of particular challenges for the Church, which receives a message with a high theological value. The text is addressed to Christians converted from paganism, to the *exiles of the dispersed tribes in Pontus, Galatia, Cappadocia, Asia and Bithynia* (1:1). Peter encourages them to *stand fast in the grace of God* (5:12) and exhorts them to dedication and patient perseverance (1:13, 4:19, 5:7-8) in the face of trials and difficulties.

Chapter 4, in particular, is divided into three sections. The first section highlights the parallel between the suffering that Christ endured in his own flesh and the sentiments that must animate Christians (vv. 1-2). The second portrays the "different" connotation of Christians in the social context in which they live (vv. 3-6). The last section begins with the eschatological perspective and focuses on the communitarian dynamics in the life of the Christians with clear and valuable directives (vv. 7-11).

The tenth verse: *Each one of you has received a special grace, so, like good stewards responsible for all these varied graces of God, put it at the service of others*, outlines the grace-filled nature of the followers of Christ and His Gospel, that is to say, the outpouring of gifts into the life of every believer. Indeed, Peter invites each person to live this gift (*chárisma*) as servants (*diakonìa*) becoming dispensers (*oikonòmoi*) of grace (4:10).

The gifts received from God are called charisms, from the Greek *charis*, which derives from the verb *charizomai*, which means: to give, to be munificent, generous, to give freely.

The term *chárisma* in the New Testament is used only in reference to gifts that come from God. Each individual charism is not a gift given to all, but a special gift that the Spirit distributes « as he wishes » (*1 Cor* 12: 11) [1].

The Christian, therefore, is called to become a treasurer, a steward of the varied graces

---

[1] Cf. CONGREGATION FOR THE DOCTRINE OF THE FAITH, Lett. *Iuvenescit Ecclesia* on the relationship between hierarchical and charismatic gifts for the life and mission of the Church, Rome (15 May 2016), 4.

8

that are expressed also through charisms and are to be made available for the benefit of all. Each gift is an enrichment of God's boundless patrimony of grace. Every member of the community, therefore, rich in this gift, is an active and co-responsible member of community life. They know that what they have is not theirs, but rather a gift to be preserved, to be made fruitful with one purpose: the common good, « because only together it is possible to reach it, increase it, and keep it, even in view of the future » [2]. The common good provides a multiplicity of gifts, at the service of one another, through which God's salvific project works for the benefit of every man and woman.

2. In God's salvific plan the Church is « like the faithful and prudent steward [who] has the task of carefully taking care of what has been entrusted to him ». In fact, « he is aware of the responsibility of protecting and managing with attention his own goods, in the light of his mission of evangelization and with particular care for the needy » [3].

[2] PONTIFICAL COUNCIL FOR JUSTICE AND PEACE, *Compendium of the Church's Social Doctrine,* Roma (2 April 2004), § 164.

[3] FRANCIS, Lett. Ap. in form of a motu proprio *Fidelis dispensator et prudens* for the constitution of a new struc-

The current historical reality calls consecrated life to take into consideration a widespread decline in vocations and a long lasting economic crisis. This situation urges us to « assume with realism, trust and hope the new responsibilities which call us to regard a world that needs a profound cultural renewal and the rediscovery of fundamental values on which to build a better future. The crisis forces us to redesign our path, to give ourselves new rules and to find new forms of involvement, to focus on positive experiences and reject the negative ones. The crisis thus becomes an *opportunity for discernment and new envisioning*. From the viewpoint that is trustful rather than resigned, can one better face the difficulty of the present moment » [4].

In this context the institutes of consecrated life and societies of apostolic life are called to be *good stewards* of the charisms received from the Spirit through the management and administration of their assets.

3. In recent years, many have faced problems of an economic nature. We could say

ture of coordination of the economic and administrative affairs of the Holy See and the State of Vatican City (24 February 2014), *incipit*.

[4] BENEDICT XVI, Encyclical Letter *Caritas in veritate* (29 June 2009), 21.

that the growing decrease in strength has been accompanied by an increase in difficulties. Insufficient preparation and lack of planning have often been the cause of economic choices that have not only endangered the assets, but the very survival of the institutes as well. The Congregation for Institutes of Consecrated Life and Societies of Apostolic Life, taking note of the situation, urged the institutes and the societies to assume a greater awareness about the relevance of the economic issues, providing criteria and practical instructions for the management of assets.

In this context the two *International Symposia* on asset management were offered. The first one, entitled *Management of Ecclesiastical Assets of Institutes of Consecrated life and Societies of Apostolic Life in Service of Humanity and the Mission of the Church*[5], took place in March 2014. Subsequent to it, the *Guidelines for the Management of the Assets in Institutes of Consecrated Life and Societies of Apostolic Life*[6]

---

[5] CONGREGATION FOR INSTITUTES OF CONSECRATED LIFE AND SOCIETIES OF APOSTOLIC LIFE, *The Management of the Goods of the Institutes of Consecrated Life and Societies of Apostolic Life at the service of humanity and of the Mission of the Church. Acts of the International Symposium (Rome, 8-9 March 2014)*, LEV, Vatican City 2014.

[6] CONGREGATION FOR INSTITUTES OF CONSECRATED LIFE AND SOCIETIES OF APOSTOLIC LIFE, Lett. circ. *Guide-*

were published on August 2, 2014. The guidelines and principles for asset management have been offered « as an aid so that the institutes may respond with renewed audacity and prophecy to the challenges of our time, to continue to be a prophetic sign of God's love » [7].

In the following period the Dicastery's attention was also directed towards the importance of the works. If the focus of the first Symposium was to review the ability to be accountable, the duty to protect the assets, and the duty of oversight and control by superiors, the second Symposium, held in November 2016, focused on the charismatic significance: *Rethinking economic matters in a manner faithful to the charism.*

4. In the wake of the rich Magisterium of Pope Francis, the current document – in continuity with the text of the *Guidelines* – proposes to:

– continue a journey of ecclesial reflection on the assets and their management, making use of the suggestions which the Dicastery received from the superiors of the

lines for the Management of Goods in Institutes of Consecrated Life and in Societies of Apostolic Life, Rome (2 August 2014).
   [7] *Ibid*, 6.

Institutes of consecrated life and of the Societies of apostolic life[8];

– to recall and explain some canonical aspects regarding temporal goods with particular reference to the practice of the Congregation for Institutes of Consecrated Life and Societies of Apostolic Life;

– suggest some tools for planning and programming with respect to the management of the works;

– urge the institutes of consecrated life and societies of apostolic life, at all levels, from superiors to members, to rethink the economic reality in a manner faithful to each charism so as to be « for the Church and for the world, the outposts of care for all of the poor and for all material, moral, and spiritual poverty, and examples in overcoming every form of egoism through the logic of the Gospel which teaches us to trust in the Providence of God »[9].

---

[8] *Ibid.*

[9] FRANCIS, *Message to the participants at the International Symposium on the theme: "Management of ecclesial goods of Institutes of Consecrated Life and Societies of Apostolic Life at the service of humanity and the mission of the Church"*, Rome (8 March 2014).

I.

LIVING MEMORY
OF THE POOR CHRIST

The poverty of Christ, the Good News of the Gospel

5. Living the good news of the Gospel «means living in a way that reflects the poverty of Christ, whose whole life was focused on doing the will of the Father and serving others»[1].

Pope Francis does not avoid opportunities to bring us continually to the core meaning of the *sequela Christi*: «The explicit desire for total conformation to Him»[2], to His life, to His *kénosi*. The mystery of the Incarnation is a mystery of poverty: *from being rich He was made poor for us* (cf. *2 Cor.* 8:9). On the cross

---

[1] FRANCIS, *Homily* during the Mass with the Bishops, Priests, and Religious, on the occasion of the Apostolic Trip in Sri Lanka and the Philippines, Manila (16 January 2015).

[2] JOHN PAUL II, Post Synod Ap. Ex. *Consecrated Life* (25 March 1996), 18

« His poverty will become being stripped of everything »[3], He experiences completely the mystery of *kénosi*, like the *suffering Servant* announced by Isaiah.

6. « Hidden in the poverty of Christ are the infinite riches of God. [He] is not only the teacher, but also the spokesman and guarantor of that saving poverty, which corresponds to the infinite wealth of God and the inexhaustible power of this grace »[4]. Therefore, *kénosi* is a fundamental criterion for the life of every baptized person and, even more so, of every consecrated person. Poverty, « lived out of the example of Christ *who became poor although He was rich* (*2 Cor.* 8:9), becomes an expression of the *total gift of Himself* which the three divine Persons are for each other. It is a gift that overflows onto creation and manifests itself fully in the Incarnation of the Word and in His redemptive death »[5].

Jesus in the synagogue of Nazareth at the beginning of his ministry, stated that *the Gospel is proclaimed to the poor* (cf. *Lk.* 4:18, *Is.* 61:1).

---

[3] *Ibid*, 23; cf. *Fil.* 2:5-11.

[4] JOHN PAUL II, Ap. Ex. *Redemptionis donum* (25 March 1984), 12.

[5] JOHN PAUL II, Post Synod Ap. Ex. *Consecrated Life* (25 March 1996), 21.

Those who want to follow him are therefore called to abandon goods, home, family, to begin their journey devoid of all (*Lk.* 14:33; 18:22). The Master asks, first of all, to welcome and therefore to live *the primacy of the Kingdom*, to which nothing can be preferred or pre-empted. This is why the poor in spirit are called blessed (*Mt.* 5:3), since they are the first recipients of the Kingdom, those who are in a position to await it, desire it, and welcome it.

7. Holy poverty is what makes persons interiorly free, and allows them to grow in faith and charity, a charity that has eyes able to see the needs of others, and to have a merciful heart to help them. Holy poverty is animated by the love that places others before itself, and puts its trust in God, who provides for His creatures every day, like the lilies of the fields and the birds of the sky (cf. *Mt.* 6:25-34).

Holy poverty is recommended by Jesus to the young man who *went away sad because he had many goods* (*Mk.* 10:22) and wanted to keep them for himself. The Master had suggested that he sell everything so as to lead him to interior freedom and to mercy that is authentic and generous. Poverty leads to charity, and thus enters into the contemplation of the mystery of God.

8. The testimony of consecrated life assumes *a moderate lifestyle.* In his Encyclical Letter *Laudato si'* on the care of the common home, Pope Francis weaves the praise of moderation: « Christian spirituality – the Pope writes – proposes a growth marked by moderation and the capacity to be happy with little. It is a return to that simplicity which allows us to stop and appreciate the small things, to be grateful for the opportunities which life affords us, to be spiritually detached from what we possess, and not to succumb to sadness for what we lack » [6]. Consecrated persons with their choice of poverty, professed by a vow or by some other sacred bond, according to their specific charism, are living and credible witnesses that « moderation, when lived freely and consciously, is liberating. It is not a lesser life, or one lived with less intensity. On the contrary, it is a way of living life to the full » [7].

The poverty of consecrated persons seeks to « witness to God as the true wealth of the human heart » [8], to confess that with

[6] FRANCIS, Encyclical Letter *Laudato si'* (24 May 2015), 222.

[7] *Ibid,* 223.

[8] JOHN PAUL II, Post Synod Ap. Ex. *Consecrated Life* (25 March 1996), 90.

Christ they possess *better and more lasting goods* (*Heb* 10:34): faith in Him gives life « a new basis, a new foundation on which man can rest » [9].

With their poverty, the consecrated bear witness to a truly human quality of life that relativizes the nature of goods by pointing to God as the absolute good [10]. The simplicity, moderation, and austerity of life of consecrated persons give them complete freedom in God [11].

Towards "the flesh of Christ"

9. « Man, and especially the poor, are exactly the path of the Church, because it was the path of Jesus Christ » [12]. The poor have always been at the center of Jesus' attention, who tried to give them dignity, life, the possibility of living their humanity to its fullness. Pope Francis, in the tradition of the Magiste-

[9] BENEDICT XVI, Encyclical Letter *Spe Salvi*, (30 November 2007), 8.

[10] Cf. JOHN PAUL II, Post Synod Ap. Ex. *Consecrated Life* (25 March 1996), 89.

[11] Cf. FRANCIS, *Discourse to the participants on the day dedicated to the pontifical representatives*, Rome (21 June 2013).

[12] J.M. BERGOGLIO, *Only Love Can Save Us*, LEV, Vatican City 2013, 113.

rium, continually states: « How I would like it to be a poor Church and for the poor » [13]. These words pronounced the day after his election can well be said to be one of the key aspects of his pontificate. « For the Church, the option for the poor is a theological category before it is cultural, sociological, political or philosophical. God grants them "His first mercy". This divine preference has consequences for the faith life of all Christians called to have *the same sentiments of Jesus* (*Phil.* 2:5) » [14].

10. This requirement to be attentive to the needs of the poor in the footsteps of the Master, was incarnated in the first community of disciples. In the *Acts of the Apostles* (cf. *Acts* 2:42-47, 4:32-37) the Church of Jerusalem is presented as an assembly in which charity and sharing of goods, distributed to *each according to need* (*Acts* 4:35), made sure that *no one of them was in need* (*Acts* 4:34). Among the constant practices of this community, in addition to being faithful to the teaching of the Apostles, the breaking of bread,

[13] FRANCIS, *Discourse to the representatives of the media*, Rome (16 March 2013); FRANCIS, Ap. Ex. *Evangelii Gaudium* (24 November 2013), 198.

[14] FRANCIS, Ap. Ex. *Evangelii Gaudium* (24 November 2013), 198.

and prayers, there is also *koinonía* (*Acts* 2:42), having *all things in common* (*Acts* 2:44, 4:32) and sharing the goods *according to the need of each one* (*Acts* 2:45).

Also, the great collection for the Mother Church of Jerusalem, organized by Paul in the Churches he founded (*1 Cor.* 16:1-4, *Rom.* 15:25-28, *2 Cor.* 8:9), is a gesture of solidarity that expands the horizon of ecclesial communion.

These texts constitute an inspirational paradigm for the way of being and acting in the communities of the disciples for every time and in every place. Christians saw themselves called to and responsible for finding suitable ways for putting the needs of *koinonía* into practice. Consecrated persons, incarnating the poverty of Christ in history and drawing inspiration from the life of the first communities, are called to make their own the urgency of *koinonía*. It is the choice to follow the poor Christ which leads to choosing on behalf of the poor.

11. «A poor Church for the poor begins by reaching out to the flesh of Christ»[15].

[15] FRANCIS, *Words on the occasion of the Pentecost Vigil with movements, new communities, associations, and ecclesial aggregations*, Rome (18 May 2013).

The contemplation of the face of the Father revealed in Jesus Christ, the concreteness of His love manifested in the Incarnation of the Son (cf. *Phil.* 2:7), leads one to discover Him in all of the poor and the marginalized. One does not only give things to the poor, it is necessary to share with them, even better, to restore what belongs to them. Consecrated men and women who have experienced the gratuitous love of the Father, are called to live the spirituality of restitution, to freely return what has been given to them for the service of their sisters and brothers: life, gifts, time, needed goods. The consecrated person seeks « a true *encounter* with the poor and provides an opportunity for *sharing* that becomes a style of life » [16]: living *sine proprio* – following the example of Francis of Assisi – thus achieving the highest degree of evangelical poverty.

Consecrated persons are called not only to personal poverty – « poverty today is a cry. All of us should think of becoming a little poorer » [17] –, but also of a community poverty; not only should the members be detached from property, but also should institutions:

[16] FRANCIS, *Message for the First World Day of the Poor*, Rome (13 June 2017), 3.

[17] FRANCIS, *Discourse to students of schools run by Jesuits in Italy and in Albania*, Rome (7 June 2013).

« Empty convents are not ours, they are for the flesh of Christ » [18]. The religious community, therefore, must stand firm on poverty, because « any Church community, if it thinks it can comfortably go its own way without creative concern and effective cooperation in helping the poor to live with dignity and reaching out to everyone, will also risk breaking down » [19].

The community is called to exercise discernment not so much to identify the categories of the poor, but rather to be close to them, whoever they may be and wherever they may meet them, to experience a poverty capable of becoming enriched *in the breadth, length, height and depth of love of Christ* (cf. *Eph.* 3:18-19).

The Human Face of Economic Systems

12. Human beings and their well-being must also have primary significance in economic activity as they more broadly have in social organization and in political life. The Constitution *Gaudium et Spes* recalled it:

[18] FRANCIS, *Discourse on the occasion of the Visit to Center "Astalli" for service to refugees,* Rome (10 September 2013).

[19] FRANCIS, Ap. Ex. *Evangelii Gaudium* (24 November 2013), 207.

« Man is in fact the author, the center, and the end of all economic-social life »[20], and Benedict XVI reiterated: « The first capital to be safeguarded and valued is man, the person, in his integrity »[21]. The economic dimension, therefore, is intimately connected with the person and the mission. Through economic systems important choices are made for the life of the individual and for the life of the collective, in which evangelical witness must be visible, attentive to the needs of the brothers and sisters.

Consecrated men and women choose to be the voice of the prophet and flee from the « dictatorship of a faceless economy without a truly human purpose »[22]. Their poverty reminds everyone of the urgency to free oneself from the economy of exclusion and inequity, because this economy kills[23]. In fact, it leads us to consider « the human being in himself as a consumer good, which can be used and then thrown away. We have started the culture of the "gap" which even promotes [...]

[20] SECOND ECUMENICAL COUNCIL VATICAN, Past. Const. on the Church in the Modern World *Gaudium et Spes*, 63.

[21] BENEDICT XVI, Let Enc. *Caritas in veritate* (29 June 2009), 25.

[22] FRANCIS, Ap. Ex. *Evangelii Gaudium* (24 November 2013), 55.

[23] Cf. *Ibid*, 53 ff.

that the excluded are not "exploited" but rather waste, "leftovers" » [24].

The evangelical credibility of consecrated persons is also linked to the way in which goods are managed. One cannot give in to the temptation of seeking the technical and organizational efficiency of material resources and works, rather than the efficacy of action in light of the Gospel. With this in mind, the major superiors must be aware that not all management techniques correspond to the principles of the Gospel and are in agreement with the social teaching of the Church [25]. « Economic structures and their management are never ethically and anthropologically neutral. Either they contribute to building relationships of justice and solidarity or they generate situations of exclusion and rejection » [26].

13. This focus on placing the person at the center, with all his/her characteristics and uniqueness, recalls the continuous challenge

[24] *Ibid*, 53.

[25] Cf. CONGREGATION FOR INSTITUTES OF CONSECRATED LIFE AND SOCIETIES OF APOSTOLIC LIFE, Lett. circ. *Guidelines for the management of goods in Institutes of Consecrated Life and in Societies of Apostolic Life*, Rome (2 August 2014), 3.

[26] FRANCIS, *Message to the participants at the second international symposium on the theme: "In fidelity to the charism re-think the economy of the Institutes of Consecrated Life and the Societies of Apostolic Life"*, Rome (25 November 2016).

to overcome a functionalist mentality even within the communities thereby demonstrating careful care and enhancement of all members, especially the elderly. It is a concrete matter of integrating our elderly into community dynamics, appealing to their resources of witness and prayer, valuing their experience and wisdom, and involving them, even at this stage, in ways of service for which they are still capable. This integration becomes a sign of contradiction in a society where even the elderly risk being set aside as waste. We know well how this dynamic of acceptance and appreciation is always present in our companionship: the institutes commit themselves to guarantee – with considerable investment of energy and goods – a dignified assistance to the elderly and sick sisters and brothers.

In the same way, consecrated elderly members are called to welcome with openness and trust the proposals of the younger brothers and sisters, so that in every community the prophecy of Joel can be realized: *your sons and daughters will prophesy, your old men will dream dreams, your young men will see visions* (3:1), without ever yielding *to the temptation of survival*[27].

---

[27] Cf. FRANCIS, *Homily* on the occasion of the Feast of the Presentation of the Lord, XXI World Day of Consecrated Life, Rome (2 February 2017).

Economic structures as an instrument of the Church's missionary action

14. Thinking about the economic structures means being part of the humanizing process, which makes us, to put it in Latin terms, *humanissimi*, a person in the fullest sense of the word, aware of oneself and of one's relationship-mission in the world: « I am a mission on this earth; that is the reason why I am here in this world » [28].

On the occasion of the first Symposium for General Treasurers, the Holy Father recalled: « The institutes of consecrated life and societies of apostolic life have always been a prophetic voice and living witness to the newness which is Christ [...]. This loving poverty is solidarity, sharing, and charity, and is expressed in moderation, in the quest for justice and in taking joy in the essential, so as to guard against the material idols which blur the authentic meaning of life » [29].

---

[28] Cf. FRANCIS, Ap. Ex. *Evangelii Gaudium* (24 November 2013), 273.

[29] FRANCIS, *Message to the participants of the International Symposium on the theme: "Management of ecclesiastical goods in Institutes of Consecrated Life and Societies of Apostolic Life at the service of humanity and the mission of the Church"*, Rome (8 March 2014).

The poverty of consecrated persons must therefore be loving action, not theory[30]. It strongly disputes the idolatry of mammon, proposing itself as a prophetic call to a society that, in so many parts of the affluent world, risks losing the sense of value and the very meaning of things. For this reason, today more than at other times, this call finds resonance with those who, aware of the limited resources of the planet, call for respect for and protection of creation through reducing consumption, frugality, and the need to rein in one's own desires.

If economic structures are an instrument, if money must serve and not govern, then it is necessary to look at the charism, at the management, the aims, the meaning, and the social and ecclesial implications of the economic choices made by the institutes of consecrated life and societies of apostolic life[31].

15. The way one approaches ecclesiastical goods determines how temporal goods are to be approached as a means to attain the de-

[30] Cf. *Ibid.*

[31] Cf. FRANCIS, *Message to the participants at the second international symposium on the theme: "In fidelity to the charism re-think the economy of Institutes of Consecrated Life and Societies of Apostolic Life"*, Rome (25 November 2016).

sired goals. In fact, the assets of the institutes are ecclesiastical goods (can. 634 § 1). Those assets belonging to public juridical persons (can. 1257 § 1) are to be used in a manner corresponding to the mission of the Church (can. 114 § 1), « to fulfill the proper function entrusted to them in view of the public good in the name of Church » (can. 116 § 1). In fact, the assets of the institutes contribute to the « same evangelical goals for promoting the human person, for mission, for charitable sharing, and for solidarity with the people of God: in particular a common lived commitment to care and have concern for the poor is capable of giving new life to the institute » [32]. As stated in the conciliar Constitution *Gaudium et Spes*, the Church uses « temporal things to the extent that their mission requires it »; and further, she « will renounce the exercise of certain legitimately acquired rights if she finds that their use creates doubt about the sincerity of her witness » [33].

The fidelity to the charism and to the mission remains, therefore, the fundamental cri-

---

[32] CONGREGATION FOR INSTITUTES OF CONSECRATED LIFE AND SOCIETIES OF APOSTOLIC LIFE, *Guidelines. New Wine in New Wineskins. The consecrated life and its ongoing challenges since Vatican II,* Rome (6 January 2017), 28.

[33] SECOND ECUMENICAL COUNCIL VATICAN, Past. Const. on the Church in the Modern World *Gaudium et Spes,* 76.

terion for evaluating the works[34], in fact « profitability cannot be the only criterion to keep in mind »[35].

The re-thinking of the economic structures must take place through careful discernment: listening to the Word of God and history. The untiring commitment to discernment will thus allow us to choose, with creative wisdom and an available heart, works that offer new dignity « to those who are marginalized, the weak and fragile: the unborn, the poorest, the elderly infirm, the seriously disabled »[36]. In the letter addressed to all consecrated persons on the occasion of the Year of Consecrated Life, Pope Francis affirmed: « I ask you to work concretely in welcoming refugees, drawing near to the poor, and finding creative ways to catechize, to proclaim the Gospel, and to teach others how to pray. Consequently, I would hope that structures can be streamlined, large religious houses repurposed for

[34] Cf. FRANCIS, *Message to the participants at the second international symposium on the theme: "In fidelity to the charism re-think the economy of Institutes of Consecrated Life and of Societies of Apostolic Life"*, Rome (25 November 2016).

[35] FRANCIS, Encyclical Letter *Laudato si'* (24 May 2015), 187.

[36] Cf. FRANCIS, *Message to the participants at the second international symposium on the theme: "In fidelity to the charism re-think the economy of Institutes of Consecrated Life and of Societies of Apostolic Life"*, Rome (25 November 2016).

works which better respond to the present demands of evangelization and charity, and apostolates adjusted to new needs»[37].

At the same time, it is important to maintain a renewed awareness that prevents a welfare mentality, which covers deficits without solving the management problems. This can result in serious harm, because it may dissipate resources that could be used in other works of charity[38].

The institutes must be concerned not only with the results of their management, but also with the whole process of the economic structure. « The Church's social doctrine has always maintained that *justice must be applied to every phase of economic activity, thus every economic decision has a moral consequence.* Hence the canons of justice must be respected from the outset, as the economic process unfolds, and not just afterwards or incidentally»[39].

---

[37] FRANCIS, *Apostolic Letter* to all the consecrated on the occasion of the Year of Consecrated Life, Rome (23 November 2014), 2.

[38] Cf. CONGREGATION FOR INSTITUTES OF CONSECRATED LIFE AND SOCIETIES OF APOSTOLIC LIFE, Lett. circ. *Guidelines for the management of the goods of Institutes of Consecrated Life and of Societies of Apostolic Life*, Rome (2 August 2014), 9, 1.1.

[39] BENEDICT XVI, Encyclical Letter *Caritas in veritate* (29 June 2009), 37.

Evangelical economic structures of sharing and communion

16. Institutes of consecrated life and societies of apostolic life are invited to seek new «ways of understanding economic structures and development»[40]. Fraternity, solidarity, the rejection of indifference, gratuity are the most basic remedies for conflicts, including economic ones, and the starting point for building a just and equitable society aimed at reflecting, as far as possible, the longed-for homeland, where there will be *a new heaven and a new earth where justice dwells* (*2Pet.* 3:13).

«If development calls for an ever-growing number of technical experts, even more necessary still is the deep thought and reflection of wise persons in search of a new humanism, one which will enable our contemporaries to enjoy the higher values of love and friendship, of prayer and contemplation, and thus find themselves. This is what will guarantee authentic human development»[41].

Development therefore – if it wants to be authentically human – must make room for charisms. The foundational charisms, in fact,

[40] FRANCIS, Encyclical Letter *Laudato si'* (24 May 2015), 16.

[41] PAUL VI, Encyclical Letter *Populorum progressio* (26 March 1967), 20.

are fully inscribed in the « logic of gift [which] does not exclude justice, nor does it merely sit alongside it as a second element added from outside » [42]. In *being-gift*, the consecrated make a real contribution to the development of both social and political economic structures, which, « if it wants to be authentically human », must « make room for the *principle of gratuity* as an expression of fraternity [...] its nature goes beyond merit; its rule is superabundance » [43]. The superabundance challenges business concepts: it is the measure of charity! « The charismatic gifts, in fact, enable the faithful to respond to the gift of salvation in complete freedom and in a way suited to the times. In this way, they themselves become a gift of love for others and authentic witnesses to the Gospel before all humankind » [44]. In fact, « in the logic of the Gospel, if one does not give all of oneself, one never gives enough of oneself » [45].

[42] BENEDICT XVI, Encyclical Letter *Caritas in veritate*, (29 June 2009), 34.

[43] *Ibid.*

[44] CONGREGATION FOR THE DOCTRINE OF THE FAITH, Lett. *Iuvenescit Ecclesia* on the relationship between hierarchical and charismatic gifts for the life and mission of the Church, Rome (15 May 2016), 15.

[45] FRANCIS, *Discourse to the participants at the meeting "Economy of communion", promoted by the Focolari Movement*, Rome (4 February 2017).

17. Consecrated life must free itself from the technocratic paradigm by fully exercising the freedom that « is the ability to limit and direct technology; and to put it at the service of another type of progress, which is healthier, more human, more social, more integral » [46].

Each is called to an ecological conversion, which commits individuals and communities: « Social problems must be addressed by community networks and not simply by the sum of individual good deeds. [...] The ecological conversion needed to bring about lasting change is also a community conversion » [47]. As a body of those in consecrated life, we are called to make this invitation our own, and to set in motion the newness of life that is present in our charisms. Even today, by increasing the special abilities that God has given to each one, we are invited to grow in creativity and enthusiasm, so as to solve the tragedies of the world, offering ourselves to God *as a living sacrifice, holy and acceptable* (*Rom.* 12:1) [48].

[46] FRANCIS, Encyclical Letter *Laudato si'* (24 May 2015), 112.

[47] *Ibid,* 219.

[48] Cf. *Ibid,* 220.

Formation for economic matters

18. With a view to a conversion of mentality and of economic and management practices, « rethinking the economy requires specific skills and abilities, [...] it is a dynamic that affects the lives of everyone. It is not a task that can be delegated to someone but calls for the full responsibility of every person »[49].

All the members of institutes of consecrated life and societies of apostolic life must accept the responsibility to see that the utmost attention is given to ensuring that the administration of economic resources is always essentially at the service of the expressed purpose of the proper charism.

The increasing complexity in the administration of goods has accentuated a tendency to avoid co-responsibility and the assigning or delegating these duties to others, if not just to a single person. This movement has generated carelessness towards economic matters within the communities. This carelessness has led to a loss of contact with the cost of living and management fatigue. This then opens

---

[49] FRANCIS, *Message to the participants at the second international symposium on the theme: "In fidelity to the charism re-think the economy of Institutes Consecrated Life and Societies Apostolic Life"*, Rome (25 November 2016).

the possible risk of having a dichotomy between economic structures and mission [50].

Formation in *economic matters* begins with sharing the human, ethical, and moral purposes of service, so as to rediscover the evangelical dimension of the economic structures. This then permits one to manage economic structures according to the principles of gratuity, fraternity, and justice, and to live the reason for the gift, thus making a real contribution to the economic, social, and political development of society and of the Church itself [51].

19. Formation helps « to enter into an explicit process of discernment, purification, and reform » [52] in concrete situations. Focusing the processes of formation on the economic dimension means to help transformation, emphasizing the need to turn towards the Lord Jesus, also with respect to economic matters, to become « witnesses of a different

[50] Cf, CONGREGATION FOR INSTITUTES OF CONSECRATED LIFE AND SOCIETIES OF APOSTOLIC LIFE, Lett. circ. *Guidelines for the management of goods in Institutes Consecrated Life and in Societies Apostolic Life*, Rome (2 August 2014), 3.

[51] Cf. *Ibid*, 5.

[52] FRANCIS, Ap. Ex. *Evangelii Gaudium* (24 November 2013), 30.

way of doing, acting, living»[53]. To this end, adequate preparation will be necessary in the light of the Social Doctrine of the Church. In fact, «placing themselves totally at the service of the mystery of Christ's love for humankind and the world, religious anticipate and show by their very lives some of the traits of the new humanity that this social doctrine seeks to encourage»[54].

Pope Francis in the Encyclical *Laudato si'* urged seminaries and religious houses of formation to provide «an education in responsible simplicity of life, in grateful contemplation of God's world, and in concern for the needs of the poor, and the protection of the environment»[55].

This leads to living an incarnated spirituality, which considers the real world as that place where God is both made manifest and is encountered, develops a contemplative attitude capable of listening to His voice in the experiences of life, so as to discover His face

---

[53] A. SPADARO, *"Wake up the World!"*. *Colloquy of Pope Francis with the Superiors General*, in: *La Civiltà Cattolica*, 165 (2014/I), 5.

[54] PONTIFICAL COUNCIL FOR JUSTICE AND PEACE, *Compendium of the Church's Social Doctrine*, Rome (2 April 2004), 540.

[55] FRANCIS, Encyclical Letter *Laudato si'* (24 May 2015), 214.

in every person, especially in the most disadvantaged. It is a spirituality that does not admit dichotomies or reductionism[56]. History and daily life are sacred places in which the Word is revealed, and then both challenges and transfigures reality.

By proposing an incarnate spirituality, the process of formation leads one to see reality from the point of view of the poor, to develop an effective compassion for them, to take responsibility for suffering, and to commit oneself to promoting justice, peace, and the integrity of creation.

Formation with respect to economic matters, consistent with the specific charism, is fundamental for permitting choices for the mission to be innovative and prophetic.

Heeding the voice of prophecy

20. « The prophets – Pope Francis affirms in the *Apostolic Letter to All Consecrated People* – receives from God the ability to scrutinize the times in which they live and to interpret events: they are like sentinels who keep watch in the night and sense the coming of the

---

[56] Cf. Congregation for Institutes of Consecrated Life and Societies of Apostolic Life, *Directives on Formazione in religious Institutes*, Rome (2 February 1990), 17.

dawn (cf. *Is.* 21:11-12) » [57]. This results in concrete responsibilities towards our social and economic environment. « Under the current uncertainties, in a society capable of mobilizing immense means but whose cultural and moral reflection is still inadequate with regard to their use in achieving the appropriate ends », consecrated persons must feel the urgency to give witness to the prophecy that invites us « not to give in. We are asked above all to build a meaningful future for the generations to come. We should not be afraid to propose new ideas ». In fact, « through a commitment of *community* imagination it is possible to transform not only institutions but also lifestyles, and to elicit a better future for all peoples » [58].

21. Some institutes of consecrated life and societies of apostolic life are implementing initiatives within their respective legal structures, which are worthy of reflection and consideration. There are new creative models of

[57] FRANCIS, *Apostolic Letter* to all consecrated persons on the occasion of the Year of Consecrated Life, Rome (23 November 2014), 2.

[58] PONTIFICAL COUNCIL FOR JUSTICE AND PEACE, Nota *For a reform of the International financial and monetary systems form the perspective of a universal competent public authority*, Rome (24 October 2011).

charity and, at the same time, of research and development of new designs supported by appropriate guidelines. In the context of these activities, the institutes and societies should together with the collaboration of experts in sharing their experiences, study which legal framework can best protect and promote the effectiveness of their services.

Today we are witnessing an acceleration in the change of laws, which brings about uncertainty and inevitably affects the already precarious situation of some works. This calls for a strengthening of the link with those centers – including academic ones – that ensure legislative monitoring and foresee the effects or impacts both medium and long-range on the activities managed by the institutes. Furthermore, it would be desirable to promote invitations to collaborate with the respective bodies of the Episcopal Conferences that coordinate various ministries (educational works, health activities, socio-health, and social assistance). Along this line, the creation of permanent commissions would help establish common approaches toward civil authorities.

II.

VIEW OF GOD:
CHARISM AND MISSION

Striving towards the Kingdom to come

22. Eschatological tension characterizes the consecrated life and, at the same time, represents its dynamism, which the mission « *Come, Lord Jesus!* (*Ap.* 22:20) clearly articulates. This expectation is anything but passive. Although directed towards the future Kingdom, it expresses itself in work and mission [...] so that the Kingdom may become present here and now [...] consecrated life is at the service of this definitive manifestation of divine glory when all flesh will see the salvation of God » [1]. The prayer *Come, Lord Jesus!* is accompanied by another: *Thy Kingdom come* (*Mt.* 6:10) [2]. In the present and in eternity, no longer one after the other but intimately connected, faith « draws the future into the pre-

---

[1] JOHN PAUL II, Post Synod Ap. Ex. *Consecrated Life* (25 March 1996), 27.

[2] Cf. *Ibid.*

sent, so that it is no longer simply a "not yet". The fact that this future exists changes the present; the present is touched by the future reality, and thus the things of the future spill over into those of the present and those of the present into those of the future »[3].

The relationship between charism and vision of the future, therefore, is constitutive of the mission of institutes of consecrated life and of societies of apostolic life[4], who are called to live their charism in the « expectation of things to come from the perspective of a present that is already given »[5]. Elaborating a vision of the future, also in the managerial aspects of the works, is the responsibility of every institute. It is a faithful commitment to affirm the presence of the Kingdom here and now: a process of ecclesial discernment for which the works are the location of that encounter.

23. The works, therefore, should not be identified with the mission: they constitute the modality in which the mission makes itself

[3] BENEDICT XVI, Encyclical Letter *Spe Salvi* (30 November 2007), 7.

[4] Cf. JOHN PAUL II, Post Synod Ap. Ex. *Consecrated Life* (25 March 1996), 27.

[5] BENEDICT XVI, Encyclical Letter *Spe Salvi* (30 November 2007), 9.

visible, presupposes it, but does not exhaust it or define it. When it does define it – as it may have happened in the past – the paradoxical result is that a future is not offered to the works. The works can change while the mission remains faithful to the initial charismatic inspiration, becoming incarnated in the present moment; the mission must be integrated with the journey of the People of God in history[6] and those working in a mission of the Church must realize it by remaining attentive to the voice of the Spirit. Under these conditions, the charism and the works that express it recover the ability to open it to the future. Otherwise even the most innovative works are likely to give immediate answers, undoubtedly effective, but not open to prophecy and, in the end, less evangelical.

The mission, in fact, inextricably consists of the *sequela Christi* and the service to children and the poor. Born of a particular experience of the Spirit, which presents and deepens an aspect of the mystery of Christ in the Church, an authentic mission must preserve a mystical dimension. If there is a disconnect between charismatic mission and the work, the work would be an image of professional-

[6] Cf. FRANCIS, Ap. Ex. *Evangelii Gaudium* (24 November 2013),130 e *infra.*

ism, of skill, but would remain devoid of real life, of love, of depth.

In this regard, the words of Pope Francis are farsighted. They call for an understanding of the personal and collective witness of the charism that by nature looks beyond, sees, and reads with God's gaze what is happening: « Our future lies in God's gaze. We need someone who, owing to his greater familiarity with the wide expanses of God's field than with the confines of his own narrow garden, is able to assure us that what our hearts aspire to is not a vain promise »[7].

The View Outward: Discernment

24. The engagement of charism with history leads to discernment; it allows us to look with the gaze of God. It is a skill to know how to look with different eyes, an ability to see things that others do not see. Charisms allow us to see possibility where others only see inadequacy.

Discernment keeps this ability to know the breadth of God's scope, prevents petty things – the *narrow garden* of which Pope Francis speaks – from becoming absolute, and the

[7] FRANCIS, *Discourse at the reunion of the Congregation for Bishops*, Roma (27 February 2014), 1.

great ones end up becoming relative or even non-existent. The gaze, therefore, translates a certain perception of history that can connect the questions emerging from human, economic, and managerial experience with the most fundamental question of faith. In this regard, the assertion of *Evangelii Gaudium* is unequivocal: « Let us also keep in mind that we should never *respond to questions that nobody asks* » [8].

Moreover, there is a need that « ways of doing things, times and schedules, language and structures can be suitably channeled for the evangelization of today's world rather than for their self-preservation » [9]. This should also be an inescapable criterion in the manner of administering and managing the institute's assets, which sometimes seems to become an individualistic rigidity of roles and respective visions and does not remain open to overcoming ineffective practices and obsolete orientations.

25. The *outward gaze* seeks to highlight a plan, that is to say, a spiritual and ecclesial experience that takes shape gradually and

---

[8] FRANCIS, Ap. Ex. *Evangelii gaudium* (24 November 2013), 155.

[9] *Ibid*, 27.

evolves into concrete terms, into action. It is not an *a priori* vision, which refers to an established set of ideas and concepts, but rather an experience that refers to times, places, and people (as required by Saint Ignatius of Loyola), and therefore not to ideological abstractions. It becomes a vision of the future, therefore, that does not impose itself on history by trying to organize it according to its own coordinates, but instead dialogues with reality, fits into the history of humanity, and takes place over time. It is a path that is taken, a journey that begins by walking.

An open vision means, at the same time, letting *oneself look* once again at the reality that surrounds one, letting oneself be questioned by it, and looking at oneself through the questions it raises. This allows consecrated life in its choices for mission and for the management of its works to fix its gaze on the essential.

The Holy Spirit, perennial source of every charism, is a communion of love between the Father and the Son. This unfolds in a double movement of the Spirit, *ad intra* and *ad extra*: the dialogue and the relationship between Father and Son, who is the Presence of God's Love in history. This dynamic becomes the driving force of consecrated life: daily returning to the task of making the continuous freshness of the charism present in history. Therefore, the relationship with history becomes necessary for the vitality of the charism, which is and remains effective insofar as it makes this intrinsic dynamic its own. The consecrated person, therefore, brings into a changing society the Love that does not change.

Planning

26. The future viability of a charism is challenged by the rapid global changes taking place (socio-economic, political, and legislative) which are evident in the complexity of the problems to be faced, including that of management. In this perspective, it is difficult to expect immediate decisions. It is more realistic to consider together which guidelines can be sustainable in the near future, provided they do not restrict themselves to our *narrow garden*. The problem is not limited to the maintenance of the works expressing the charism, but expands to their socio-ecclesial significance, or, in other words, their evangelical efficacy.

For this purpose, it is urgent to acquire a mindset of planning. This will first of all lead to a way of proceeding and the development of tools which can anticipate, outline, and guide change and growth in daily operations. They can offer people, communities, and works the ability to look beyond, to interpret the world and current needs. It involves developing strategies and analytic techniques, assessing the real feasibility of a project. Further it includes acquiring and enhancing the institute's knowledge of projects and work done in the past, but also involving external experts, trying to learn about good practices of other institutes, bringing together the skills and abilities to work in networks. The planning mentality starts from the spiritual and ecclesial experience and from there makes real the vision of the future of the institute through a strategic plan of action, which makes use of shared approaches.

27. More effort is needed so that the path taken in recent years may make the charismatic dimension in the works and their management more visible. Recently several institutes of consecrated life and societies of apostolic life, drawing from their extended history have developed charismatically inspired documents, which find origin in lived reality. These documents have proposed a re-reading of the legislative and management standards inherent in their works, in light of the essential elements of the foundational charism.

They have reconfigured elements with an organic vision, which gives direction to economic, managerial, and financial services. This restructuring is made evident as well in some fundamental outcomes, expressive of the charism itself. For example, the outcomes seek to verify the presence of a lived *diakonia* of charity in the ongoing testimony of the charismatic values of the institute, as well as in the evaluation of the objectives and expected outcomes. The aforementioned documents – often the result of patient and laborious editing – could also be adopted by other families of consecrated life. Sharing experiences and insights is the fruitful starting point for processes of discernment concerning the reorganization of works to « safeguard the sense of one's own charism »[10].

The ecclesial significance of charisms

28. With a vision of the future, the expression of the ecclesial nature of the charism is important. This is a dimension strongly emphasized by Pope Francis: charisms « are meant to renew and build up the Church. They are not an inheritance, safely secured

[10] JOHN PAUL II, Post Synod Ap. Ex. *Consecrated Life* (25 March 1996), 63.

and entrusted to a small group for safekeeping; rather they are gifts of the Spirit integrated into the body of the Church [...]. A sure sign of the authenticity of a charism is its ecclesial character, its ability to be integrated harmoniously into the life of God's holy and faithful people for the good of all. [...] To the extent that a charism is better directed to the heart of the Gospel, its exercise will be more ecclesial » [11].

Two aspects deserve to be emphasized. Charisms are not a safely secured inheritance. The authentic sign of their ecclesial nature is the « ability to be integrated harmoniously into the life of God's holy and faithful people » [12].

Keeping the charisms alive involves vigilant safeguarding of the ecclesial nature of the gift: a charism is renewed over time so as to contribute to the building up of the Church! [13].

29. « The mission of consecrated life is universal, and many institutes embrace a global mission, but it is incarnated in specific

[11] FRANCIS, Ap. Ex. *Evangelii Gaudium* (24 November 2013), 130.
[12] *Ibid.*
[13] Cf. *Ibid*, 130-131.

local situations » [14]. The assets of the institutes of consecrated life and societies of apostolic life, in fact, do not only have meaning within the context of the local Church. In addition, their use over time is available to the universal dimensions of the Church's mission: from addressing all forms of poverty, to projects of solidarity in mission territories, and, not to be forgotten: in the formation of their candidates and the care of the elderly.

Consecrated life, nonetheless, is part of the diocesan family [15]. For this reason the appropriate autonomy – which is the duty of the local Ordinaries to conserve and protect (cf. can. 586 § 2) – cannot disregard the diocesan pastoral plan or elude prior consultation with the bishop, before proceeding with the closure of works. « Today more than ever, it is necessary to live out a just autonomy and exemption, in the institutes that have them, in strict relationship with insertion, so

[14] CONGREGATION FOR INSTITUTES OF CONSECRATED LIFE AND SOCIETIES OF APOSTOLIC LIFE, Lett. circ. *Guidelines for the management of goods of Institutes of Consecrated Life and in Societies of Apostolic Life*, Rome (2 August 2014), 16, 2.1.

[15] Cf. SACRED CONGREGATION FOR RELIGIOUS AND SECULAR INSTITUTES - SACRED CONGREGATION FOR BISHOPS, directive Criteria on the relationship between Bishops and Religious in the Church *Mutuae Relationes*, Rome (14 May 1978), 18.

that charismatic freedom and the catholicity of Consecrated Life are also expressed in the context of the particular Church. It would not fully respond to what Jesus desired for His Church were she to be deprived of Consecrated Life, which is part of her fundamental structure, in the same way that the laity or the ordained ministry is. It is for this reason that, in the light of the Second Vatican Council, we speak today of the *co-essentiality* of hierarchical and charismatic gifts (cf. *LG* 4), which flow from the one Spirit of God and nourish the life of the Church and her missionary action » [16].

30. Diocesan Bishops, for their part, are called to appreciate consecrated persons as « *a living memorial of Jesus' way of living and acting*» [17], instead of seeing them in terms of utility and functionality. They should develop a better understanding of the universality of

[16] FRANCIS, *Discourse to the participants at the International Congress for episcopal Vicars and Delegates for consecrated life*, Rome (28 October 2016), 1; cf. CONGREGATION FOR THE DOCTRINE OF THE FAITH, Lett. *Iuvenescit Ecclesia* on the relationship between hierarchical and charismatic gifts for the life and mission of the Church, Rome (15 May 2016), 10.

[17] JOHN PAUL II, Post Synod Ap. Ex. *Consecrated Life* (25 March 1996), 22.

the service of consecrated men and women and grow in collaboration with them. « Pastors are called to respect, without manipulating, the multidimensionality that constitutes the Church and through which the Church manifests itself » [18].

It is essential to begin from a theological perspective of communion so as to fully understand openness to the universal Church and, at the same time, the need and commitment to collaborate with the local Church. When communion is not a presupposition of every ecclesial relationship, we risk falling into the approach of seeking one's own desires. It is therefore necessary to promote relationships based on the principle of communion, which is based on *fraternity* and in *working together.*

Charisms: the ability to enculturate

31. Fraternal love is the key concept that best expresses the authentic contribution of consecrated life for the building up of the Church. In fact, charisms manifest their evangelical authenticity in love for one another,

---

[18] FRANCIS, *Discourse to the participants at the International Congress for episcopal Vicars and Delegates for consecrated life,* Rome (28 October 2016), 1.

and within the lives of communities. The Social Doctrine of the Church urgently invites us to find ways to put this love for one another into practice as the guiding principle of our economic order. Where other ways of thinking speak only of solidarity, the Social Doctrine of the Church speaks of fraternal love, since a fraternal society is also supportive, while the opposite is not always true, as so many experiences confirm.

Love for one another, therefore, is « a lifestyle which includes the capacity for living together and communion. Jesus reminded us that we have God as our common Father and that this makes us brothers and sisters. Fraternal love can only be gratuitous; it can never be a means of repaying others for what they have done or will do for us »[19]. In this sense « we must regain the conviction that we need one another, that we have a shared responsibility for others and the world »[20].

Responsibility also means entering into viewing management in a new way that respects and enhances the efforts of the local Church.

[19] FRANCIS, Encyclical Letter *Laudato si'* (24 May 2015), 228.

[20] *Ibid*, 229.

It is a way of operating that one attains through a shared dialogue and the elaboration of criteria for the protection and promotion of the Church's patrimony. This patrimony goes beyond the real estate and includes the experiences, the knowledge, the skills, the professionalism that have developed apostolates both large and small, both in the past and in the present: a history that has interpreted the needs and cares of local Churches.

32. Today it is no longer possible to think in isolation, as if the problems generated by the management of the works are exclusively a problem of the institutes of consecrated life and of the societies of apostolic life. Here we highlight a historically understandable situation: religious have always spoken in terms of "our" works and the local Churches have considered them the "works of the religious".

In today's ecclesial context, one has to change the way of thinking: together with other Church entities we are committed to seek possible solutions which guarantee the ecclesial dimension of our works, as well as address the concrete problem of maintaining good oversight. Therefore, the conclusion is that the journey of conversion is a communal itinerary. The future of the works concerns us as Church and further must be addressed by the Church.

The capacity to integrate oneself into the Church is fundamental to the works created to respond to the needs of the people. The problem of integration today translates into *working together*. « It inspires one to cooperate, to share, to prepare the ground for relationships governed by a common sense of responsibility. This path opens the field to new policies, new ways, new attitudes. [...] "Working together" means, in fact, basing the work not on the isolated genius of one individual, but on the co-operation of many. It means, in other words, "creating a network" in order to take advantage of everyone's gifts without, however, overlooking each person's distinct uniqueness. [...] to take courageous steps in order that "being and working together" is not merely a slogan but a program for the present and the future » [21]. This invitation to collaborate also applies to institutes of consecrated life and societies of apostolic life who are urged to « go out with greater courage from the confines of their institute to elabo-

[21] FRANCIS, *Discourse to the entrepreneurs meeting Confindustria*, Rome (27 February 2016).

rate together, locally and globally, on common projects of formation, evangelization, and social services» [22].

33. *Working together* also involves coordination and sharing in planning, management, ways of thinking, culture, and procedures, which, if done properly, could guarantee the stability of many works, as well as their evangelical efficacy and economic sustainability. Effectiveness testifies to the gospel of charity; sustainability reveals a Church that creates a network of solidarity for promoting reliable services of good quality.

A solidarity network is sustained not just by the quality of what is offered, but above all by its reliability. It is a patrimony of values in which we combine: *credibility*, cohesion, and coherence of a vision in planning and management; *professionalism*, attentive and open to learning but not solely for effectiveness or efficiency; and *experience*, cognizant of its past performance, but at the same time open to innovation and creativity.

Reliability reconfigures the hierarchy of preferences and therefore the importance of

---

[22] FRANCIS, *Apostolic Letter* to all consecrated persons on the occasion of the Year of Consecrated Life, Roma (23 November 2014), 2.

recognition and how one compares with others. Today we must invest more in a culture of the ecclesial relationship that always seeks to assure that a variety of participants remain involved in our activity in the awareness that the plurality of subjects is involved in our situations more than we are involved in the reality of integration.

III.

ECONOMIC DIMENSION
AND MISSION

The sustainability of the works

34. « The urgent challenge to protect our common home includes a concern to bring the whole human family together to seek a sustainable and integral development, for we know that things can change » [1]. In the current historical context, the institutes of consecrated life and societies of apostolic life accept the challenges that are found today: identifying prophetic responses for a careful and respectful economic and human development. The evolution of needs and the different cultural, social, and regulatory contexts often require, on one hand, the abandonment of inadequate ways of functioning and on the other, a bold and creative approach to « rethinking goals, structures, and style » [2].

[1] FRANCIS, Encyclical Letter *Laudato si'* (24 May 2015), 13.

[2] FRANCIS, Ap. Ex. *Evangelii Gaudium* (24 November 2013), 33.

Pope Francis in his message addressed to the participants of the Second Symposium organized by the Congregation for Institutes of Consecrated Life and Societies of Apostolic Life, recalled that « to be faithful commits us to an assiduous work of discernment, so that the works, consistent with the charisms, continue to be effective instruments to make God's tenderness reach many. [...] An act of courage is often required to be faithful to the charism: it is not about selling everything or of 'divesting' all the goods, but of undertaking a serious discernment [...] the discernment might suggest keeping alive a work that causes losses – being well aware that these are not generated by incapacity or unskillfulness » [3].

To evaluate the sustainability of the works, it is necessary to adopt a method that considers every aspect and all the possible interrelations, taking into consideration the charismatic, relational, and economic dimensions both of each work and of the whole institute.

[3] FRANCIS, *Message to the participants at the second international symposium on the theme: "In fidelity to the charism re-think the economy of Institutes of Consecrated Life and Societies of Apostolic Life"*, Rome (25 November 2016).

35. *Charismatic dimension and planning.* « It is necessary, therefore, to undertake a review of the mission as an expression of the charism to verify if the charismatic identity of the established works continues to emerge in the current operational activities. [...] It may happen, in fact, that works are no longer managed in a manner consistent with the current expression of the mission, and properties are no longer run as works which express the charism »[4]. It is necessary to define which « works and activities it should continue, which should be eliminated or modified, and which new frontiers it should begin to pursue and demonstrate as responding to today's need in full fidelity to its own charism »[5].

It is necessary to overcome the mentality that considers the designing and planning of activities and works to be antithetical to openness to the creativity of the Spirit. On the contrary, many intuition fail to see the light because they are not supported by a detailed proposal and/or planning: the objectives

---

[4] CONGREGATION FOR INSTITUTES OF CONSECRATED LIFE AND SOCIETIES OF APOSTOLIC LIFE, Lett. circ. *Guidelines for the management of goods in Institutes of Consecrated Life and in Societies of Apostolic Life*, Rome (2 August 2014), 8, 1.1.

[5] *Ibid.*

are not defined, nor are the means to accomplish the task identified nor the economic-financial feasibility verified. All this risks provoking a gap between ideals and achievable ends, between mission and economic structures, leading to making incorrect judgments and evaluations, to adopting ineffective measures.

The need to design and plan cannot, in any way, be interpreted as limiting ideals, or as constraining creativity. It does not imply a lack of trust in Providence, but rather the contrary. When the charismatic goal is articulated, the economic structures place themselves at the service of prophecy by means of concrete and effectively designed projects.

36. *Relational dimension and fraternal love.* As mentioned above, it is essential to rediscover economic structures with a human face, where humanity and its true goodness never loses its central role. Attention to placing the dignity of every human person and the common good[6] at the center recalls the need for positive relationships. In the richness of relationships, which constitute fraternal love, consecrated persons experience how the mis-

---

[6] Cf. FRANCIS, Ap. Ex. *Evangelii Gaudium* (24 November 2013), 203.

sion consists of people willing to share life and faith, to experience community and collaboration. Reciprocal relationships, based on sincere esteem and mutual trust, thus become valuable resources for management.

In this way, the works will be managed in a spirit of openness, community, and co-responsibility, even when their care must be entrusted to a few consecrated men and women. On the other hand, in some cases the responsibility is entrusted to some individuals, without establishing clear structures for interaction and accountability. This can lead to a personalization of management, even unwittingly, based on their talents, uniqueness, and sensibilities, thereby limiting the establishment of ways to respond to various situations that may arise. It often happens that we do not worry about the formation of those who may assume the responsibility of management and give the appropriate direction to the work.

The design and/or planning, which flows from mutual listening, allows a coherent vision for the works and for the response to the articulated needs. Further, it offers the possibility of overcoming the drive towards self-reference. When divisions and differences are overcome, advantageous solutions are found that are enriching for and shared by everyone. It is a matter of disassociating from the ideology of *homo-oeconomicus*, insatiable in its desire for goods, whose choices are determined by the maximization of personal interest. It acknowledges the challenge of *homo-fraternus*, who never tires of choosing fraternal love [7].

37. *Charisms and economic activity.* The balanced budget of works of the institutes of consecrated life and of the societies of apostolic life cannot be the only criterion to be considered in discernment regarding the sustainability of the works. However, it is necessary to remember that there is no contradiction between charism and the management of goods; managing according to economic principles does not stifle the charism, but rather allows it to pursue and achieve shared objectives. Ensuring continuity and vitality of the charism does not imply operating with superficiality and inexperience. The experience of the Dicastery shows that where insufficient attention is paid to management problems, the result is the nullification of the mission itself.

[7] Cf. *Ibid*, 91.

Consecrated life offers the world an evangelical witness when it keeps alive the apostolic inspiration and guarantees the sustainability of the works through their informed and balanced management.

Stable patrimony (assets)

38. For the purpose of orderly and far-sighted stewardship, a general survey of the institute's assets should be undertaken so as to comply with the norms established by canon law aimed at ensuring the subsistence of the institute and facilitating the attainment of its institutional aims (so-called *stable patrimony*). Hence, it is opportune to promptly take appropriate steps to inventory the assets ascribed to the stable patrimony, and where necessary, add items that should be included in the inventory, if this has not yet been done.

To this end, the proper law of each institute is asked to establish by a specific resolution the competent authority to undertake this task. This provision must appear in the fundamental code or in another normative document of proper law, with the following text or one of similar tenor: *The stable patrimony consists of all the immovable and movable property that by means of a specific assignment are destined to guarantee the economic security of the institute. For the goods of the entire institute, the General Chapter or the General Superior with the consent of his/her Council makes this assignment. For the assets of a province, as well as for the assets of a legitimately established house, the Provincial Chapter or other similar assemblies (cf. can. 632), or the Provincial Superior with the consent of his/her Council and confirmed by the Superior General makes this assignment.*

39. The stable patrimony, consisting of assets, property or furnishings, guarantees the existence of the institute, of the legitimately established provinces, of houses, and of its members. Further, it ensures the realization of the institute's mission. The stable attribute is understood as a guarantee that the work must be coherent with « an end corresponding to the mission of the Church » (can. 114 §§ 1-2) and to the specific mission of the respective institutes of consecrated life and societies of apostolic life[8].

The following can legitimately be assigned to the stable patrimony:

a) real estate, such as, for example, the places where the works function, the community houses, the residences for the elderly or

[8] Cf. JOHN PAUL II, Post Synod Ap. Ex. *Consecrated Life* (25 March 1996), 4; 72.

sick members, the assets which are particularly relevant from a historical-artistic perspective, or which are part of the beginnings or of the memory of the institute itself, like the motherhouse. The size of these assets should be proportionate to the management capacity of the institute, the province, or the religious house;

b) real estate that provides income for the support of the institute, the province or the religious house. These are the so-called income-generating assets, established to allow the legal entity to subsist or to supplement ordinary income. In these cases, it must be avoided that these goods become the reason that the legal entity exists or profits;

c) movable property that provides income for the support of the institute, of the province or of the religious house and for the realization their respective missions. These assets are fixed and legitimately assigned to the stable patrimony. These are not goods that serve the ordinary economic operations, but rather are capitalized movable assets invested in different forms in the financial system, according to the directives detailed in § 84;

d) the immovable and movable property which, having historical, artistic or intrinsic value, constitute the so-called cultural heritage, the historical memory of the institute, of the province or of the religious house. These assets may be in the form of a dowry but could also be an economic reserve for ongoing upkeep of property;

e) the protection and security fund, proportionate to the works of the institute, province, or religious house, provides appropriate protection for the institute in the presence of complex operations that may expose it to significant economic risks (so-called *emergency fund*).

40. In choosing the assets to be included in the stable patrimony, it is necessary to consider what the assets are without which the juridical person would not have the means to reach its end. Further, it is also necessary to evaluate the amount and the nature of the assets appropriate to the purpose and the needs of the same juridical person. One must take into consideration that certain assets are by their nature unavailable, as use of them may risk the loss of the same juridical person. Further, it is not permitted to proceed with the assignment of the stable patrimony for the sole purpose of avoiding the requirements of the canon law on alienation. In fact, the establishment of this patrimony is for the purpose of protecting and guaranteeing these very assets.

For the proper management of the assets assigned to the stable patrimony, it is necessary to draw up an accurate inventory of the real estate assets of the institute, of the province or of the religious house, specifying the registry data, the origin of the buildings, the presence of any restrictions, the value of the assets, and their maintenance condition. It is encouraged to review periodically the terms and conditions for the leasing of buildings or parts thereof to third parties. It is useful to keep a list of the properties and furniture that have historical, artistic, or intrinsic value. Finally, it is always necessary to ensure that the management of the assets assigned to the stable patrimony continues to be consistent with the institute's mission, so that it will not be burdened with assets or obligations unrelated to the mission. In this line, stable is not synonymous with unassailable. The inevitable volatility in the economic-financial systems suggests evaluating periodically (according to what are considered to be reasonable timeframes) the individual assets included in the patrimony.

Responsibility, transparency and trust

41. Responsibility, transparency, and the maintenance of trust are interconnected principles: no responsibility is given without transparency, transparency generates trust, trust verifies both.

Responsibility is the principle of awareness that relates the evangelizing mission to the Church's assets.

The awareness of the factors at stake provides the essential conditions for making targeted choices and eventually improving them or even changing them radically. Above all, the careful and timely accounting of the outcomes of management makes it possible to adopt the necessary corrective measures before irreversible negative consequences occur. On the contrary, an inappropriately monitored economic effort wastes resources, betraying the fundamental desire of the Church to use the assets for the common good that « must be served in its fullness, not according to reductionist visions that are subordinated by certain people to their advantage; rather it is to be based on a logic that leads to the assumption of greater responsibility »[9].

[9] PONTIFICAL COUNCIL FOR JUSTICE AND PEACE, *Compendium of the Church's Social Doctrine*, Rome (2 April 2004), 167.

Responsibility is one's obligations to the civil and ecclesial community, and above all to the respective institute. It is therefore a responsibility to recognize on the one hand, to whom one must respond, and, on the other hand, the ability to exert one's management options. Last, but not least, supervision and control are parts of this responsibility. These should not be understood as limiting the autonomy of institutions or as a lack of trust, but rather as representing a means for communication and transparency and providing protection for those who perform delicate administrative tasks [10].

42. With respect to what was previously stated: the term "transparency" refers to the ability to report on the activities, the choices made, and the results achieved. Accountability and financial statements – which are transparency tools – allow you to have a concise, but at the same time, rigorous report on the activities carried out and their results, providing the directors the ability to account for their actions, their choices, and moreover,

[10] Cf. CONGREGATION FOR INSTITUTES OF CONSECRATED LIFE AND SOCIETIES OF APOSTOLIC LIFE, Lett. circ. *Guidelines for the management of goods of Institutes of Consecrated Life and Societies of Apostolic Life*, Rome (2 August 2014), 10, 1.2.

their behavior. Regular accountability of management also fosters prudence in the administration of assets. In fact, greater awareness corresponds to greater precision in identifying risks and, where appropriate, new directions to pursue.

From this perspective we can well understand the intrinsic correlation between responsibility and transparency. The emphasis does not only concern the specific duties (superiors, treasurers/bursars, collaborators) but also – as mentioned above – the ability to communicate the reasons/motivations that guide management and management decisions, as well as the corresponding commitment to respond to problems or critical issues that may arise.

The rules of transparency, as is seen today, are imposed by civil laws with increasing intensity and importance so as to guarantee the correct and legal functioning of any entity whatever, as well as the economic sustainability of the institute's works. It must be added that these rules are becoming more complex and precise. It therefore obliges the presence of professional skills and appropriate procedures. This should not only exist at the level of the single operative unit, but, when it comes to more complex structures, at national and international levels.

43. Accountability and financial statements help to increase the credibility of the person who puts them in place and, therefore, help to increase trust. And «without rules there cannot be trust»[11], namely trust is generated as well by rules that identify responsibilities and call for transparency. Trust capital cannot be compromised by situations or events that weaken the credibility of institutes of consecrated life and societies of apostolic life in the civil and ecclesial community, thereby making "problematic" the personal and collective witness of consecrated poverty. In fact, a culture and practice of transparency is an aspect of fidelity to one's own history and charismatic practice of the vow of poverty accompanied by appropriate legislation regarding dependence on the community, and the limitation of use and disposition of goods (cf. can. 600). The relationship between the recognition of trust and the adoption of financial and budget reporting results in a communal experience: the more there is transparency of management, the more the possibility and availability of both public and private resources increases.

---

[11] PONTIFICAL COUNCIL FOR JUSTICE AND PEACE, *Note of the Holy See on finance and development on the vigil of the Conference promoted by the United Nations General Assembly at Doha* (18 November 2008), 3c.

Maintenance of Records

44. The Code of Canon Law, canon 1283 and 1284, urges an orderly conservation of the documents and prescribes, for the purposes of efficient administrative, and accounting procedures, the preparation and constant updating of the inventory of goods and property received, a careful cataloging and conservation of documents, in particular accounting records and securities against risk. The archives, if well managed, are a useful tool for verifying initiatives undertaken in the short, medium, and long term. Therefore, it is necessary to establish procedures for acquiring documents, ordering them organically, and distinguishing them thematically. It is necessary to communicate to each administrator of ecclesiastical assets the responsibilities regarding the custody of the documentation according to canonical requirements.

The inventory of assets should record the purchase, construction, donation or other civil act or business that adds to the assets, changes the condition, or divests the asset. In particular, all documents proving the legal ownership of buildings and furnishings must be kept. The documentation appropriate to a business office makes it possible to know the administrative procedures of an institute; to provide for adequate planning that considers resources; to prove the legal rights in case of disputes; to operate in administrative transparency; to preserve historical memory; and to study the way in which the charism has been realized over time. In this regard, within the archives of an ecclesial entity it is sometimes necessary to acquire, where possible, data management systems reflecting modern technologies. Taking advantage of these technologies, it is also advisable to keep a copy of the documents of considerable value in a separate protected place, in order not to lose all the documentation in the event of some disastrous occurrence [12].

The four principles of *Evangelii Gaudium*

45. In the light of the criteria that Pope Francis has offered to the whole Church in the Apostolic Exhortation *Evangelii Gaudium*, some themes can be identified concerning a management inspired by the charisms of the institutes of consecrated life and societies of apostolic life, which « can guide the develop-

[12] Cf. PONTIFICAL COMMISSION FOR THE CULTURAL GOODS OF THE CHURCH, *The Pastoral function of the ecclesiastical archives*, Vatican City (2 February 1997).

ment of life in society and the building of a people where differences are harmonized within a shared pursuit» [13].

46. *Time is greater than space* [14]. The Holy Father often refers to «starting processes» [15]. Consecrated life is called to initiate processes, it is called to new planning. «For many years we have been tempted to believe, and many have grown up with the idea that religious families should occupy spaces rather than start processes, and this is a temptation. We have to start processes, not occupy spaces» [16]. A first characteristic of all the manifestations of a charism is that they are not primarily economic, seeking to take spaces of power, but rather are expressions of an ideal, of a looking beyond, capable of understanding the needs of men and women, especially the smallest and most fragile and seeking to respond to them through a creative approach. If the charisms that burst into history represent a process of spiritual, human, eco-

[13] FRANCIS, Ap. Ex. *Evangelii Gaudium* (24 November 2013), 221.

[14] *Ibid*, 225.

[15] FRANCIS, *Discourse to priests and consecrated persons on the occasion of the pastoral Visit to Milan,* Milan (25 March 2017).

[16] *Ibid.*

nomic, and civil change, it should be noted that this process takes place through the manifestation of a charism in the present and over time.

It is a matter of honoring and patiently accompanying the beginning of processes, of looking beyond with visions of the future regardless of immediate results, to which even the sense of responsibility and the best intentions could lead. « Space – underlines the encyclical *Lumen fidei* – hardens processes, whereas time propels towards the future and encourages us to go forward in hope » [17].

47. *Reality is more important than the idea* [18]. « Today, reality challenges us – I repeat – reality invites us to be a bit of yeast, a little pinch of salt. [...] A blessed minority, which is invited again to leaven, to raise in harmony with what the Holy Spirit has inspired in the hearts of your founders and in your own hearts. This is what it takes today » [19].

Pope Francis reiterates forcefully and clearly the importance of reality. An idea is

[17] FRANCIS, Let. Enc. *Lumen fidei* (29 June 2013), 57.

[18] FRANCIS, Ap. Ex. *Evangelii Gaudium* (24 November 2013), 231-233.

[19] FRANCIS, *Discourse to priests and consecrated persons on the occasion of the pastoral Visit to Milan*, Milan (25 March 2017).

the result of a theoretical process that can always risk falling into sophism, detaching itself from the real. Sometimes even our institutes through the formulation of logical and clear proposals or documents, perhaps even captivating ones, risk deviating from what they are and from the people to whom they are sent. In fact, sometimes, we let ourselves be dazzled by the novelty of initiatives, or new structures and forget that the most important change depends on us and our desire and ability to make it happen. The intention of the incarnation (*1Jn.* 4:2) is the guiding criterion of this principle.

The works of our institutes find their origins by listening to God calling them to meet the needs of real people. They do not arise from abstract drawings on the table, but rather they are a concrete response to the needs of people whose life, history, and difficulties are known to us. In particular, when we re-read the historical origins of the institutes of consecrated life and societies of apostolic life, the link between the inspiration of the charism and the reception of the least, the poor, and the excluded is almost inseparable.

Consecrated life is called to respond today to the questions that history poses. Often this happens through simple experiences:

we listen to life, out of which intuitions are born, and which always include a charge of truth, and through this our projects arise. It is always life that comes first, it is life that is "heard and respected", with a note of humility.

48. *The whole is superior to the part*[20]. We are called to broaden our gaze to always recognize the greatest good. Consecrated life cannot withdraw into itself, it must not allow itself to be obsessed by finite and specific matters. It must acknowledge the greatest good that will bring benefits to all.

This principle must be understood according to the image of the polyhedron which consists of diversity. These intrinsic differences need to be supported by a culture of dialog as a challenging way to find the common desire: we are invited to discover links and relationships in aspects that are not homogeneous on various levels (from local to global) and in different spheres of experience (from material to spiritual). This involves learning to work together, among communities, among institutes and congregations, with the laity, with all those who seek what is good.

[20] *Ibid*, 234-237.

Consecrated life can help the local Church to open up to the dynamism of universality, and at the same time open itself to the spirit of the local Church where they live and carry out their apostolate, avoiding falling into the temptation that «the part (our small part or vision of the world) may be superior to the ecclesial whole»[21].

49. *Unity prevails over conflict, diversity*[22]. We are called to accept conflicts, willing to get our hands dirty in addressing them without being trapped by them, so as to transform them into new processes that provide for community even with its inherent differences, which must be accepted as such. «Communion also consists in confronting together and in a united fashion the most pressing questions of our day, such as life, the family, peace, the fight against poverty in all its forms, religious freedom, and education. In particular, New Movements and Communities are called to coordinate their efforts in caring for those wounded by a globalized

[21] FRANCIS, *Discourse to priests and consecrated persons on the occasion of the Pastoral visit in Milan*, Milan (25 March 2017).

[22] FRANCIS, Ap. Ex. *Evangelii Gaudium* (24 November 2013), 223-230.

mentality which places consumption at the center, neglecting God and those values which are essential for life »[23].

Solidarity, understood in its deepest and most challenging sense, thus becomes a historical construct, a vital component where conflicts, tensions, and opposites can reach a multidimensional unity that generates new life. It does not mean aiming at syncretism, or absorbing one into the other, but at a resolution on a higher level that preserves in itself the precious potential of the contrasting polarities.

[23] FRANCIS, *Discourse* to the participants at the III World Congress of ecclesial movements and of new communities, Rome (22 November 2014).

IV.

OPERATIONAL RECOMMENDATIONS

50. In the administration of goods and in the management of works, discernment « looks at the direction, the purposes, the meaning, and the social and ecclesial implications of the economic choices of the institutes of consecrated life »[1]. From this perspective, the context for reflecting upon this reality and some fundamental criteria have been identified for this task of discernment.

The important contexts in which economic activities are inserted are: an economy that has the human being in mind, the whole person and especially the poor; the explanation of economic structures as an instrument of the Church's missionary action; and – finally – an evangelical economic structure of sharing and community.

These horizons are embodied in some fundamental criteria.

---

[1] FRANCIS, *Message to the participants at the second international symposium on the theme: "In fidelity to the charism re-think economy in the Institutes of Consecrated Life and Societies of Apostolic Life"*, Rome (25 November 2016).

51. *Fidelity to God and to the Gospel.* Every consecrated life gives primacy to God, in the *sequela Christi*. Every consecrated man and woman must first of all focus on Him, contemplate Him, learn from Him, imitate Him, follow Him, the chaste poor and obedient One, so as to be faithful proclaimers of the Good News. This is why « the gift of listening: to listen to God, that with Him we may hear the cry of the people; to listen to the people until breathing in the will to which God calls us »[2] is so indispensable.

Fidelity to the charism. Every charism « is always a living reality » called to « be developed in creative fidelity »[3]. Fidelity to the charism is, therefore, the harmony between the real choices in a given situation and the core identity of the institute.

Poverty. A « responsible austerity »[4], a « healthy humility and a happy sobriety »[5] favor distancing from the perception of assets be-

[2] FRANCIS, *Discourse on the occasion of the Prayer Vigil in preparation for the Synod on the family,* Rome (4 October 2014).

[3] FRANCIS, *Message to the participants at the second international symposium on the theme: "In fidelity to the charism re-think economy in the Institutes of Consecrated Life and Societies of Apostolic Life",* Rome (25 November 2016).

[4] *Ibid.*

[5] *Ibid.*

ing owned, in favor of expressing the use of one's assets in the context of developing a special willingness to hear « the cry of the poor, of the everlasting poor and of the new poor » [6].

Respect for the ecclesiastical nature of goods. The assets of the institutes of consecrated life and of the societies of apostolic life are ecclesiastical goods (can. 634 § 1) destined to the attainment of the purposes of the Church (can. 1254). In their use the institutes, therefore, are called to safeguard their nature and to observe the respective canonical discipline.

The sustainability of the works. The works of the institutes are by nature situated in social and economic systems. A work is therefore sustainable when it maintains a balanced approach to financial matters and makes the most of available resources.

The need for reporting. Reporting is a way of acting that openly shares choices, actions, and results. The legitimate autonomy of the institutes includes, therefore, the responsibility for management decisions and how they are carried out, always abiding by the requirements of universal and proper law.

[6] *Ibid.*

52. In concrete situations, the criteria for discernment are found in the specific and *healthy traditions* of each institute, and in the unique requirements of each *legal and social context.*

The dimensions and the organization of structures, the nature of the activities, the territorial scope of operations, the applicable legal requirements, and modes of relationship between State and Church are elements that distinguish, sometimes significantly, differences among the individual institutes of consecrated life and the societies of apostolic life. Therefore, such differences must be considered, not by abandoning the foundational criteria, but rather by allowing these criteria to take historical form in the various situations.

53. With respect to the management of assets, the organizational structures of individual institutes of consecrated life and societies of apostolic life have particular importance. The institutes ordinarily possess the operational assets of the communities. However, with reference to the works there are very different models, often regulated by the different modes of relationship between State and Church, by the specific demands of the nature of similar works, and/or by the size of the activity. Thus, while in some cases the works are owned by institutes of consecrated life and the societies of apostolic life, in other cases they exist as distinct legal entities, often organized as foundations or societies.

54. The requirements of the *civil laws* that apply to individual institutes of consecrated life and societies of apostolic life and to their provinces or parts of the institute equivalent to them (cf. can. 620) cannot be disregarded. The reference made by canon law to the civil laws governing contracts (can. 1290) and, last but not least, the use of contractual instruments between the State and the Church reinforces the observance of civil laws in the same manner that one observes canon law (can. 22).

The need to safeguard the foundational criteria and the need to consider the specific situation suggest operational procedures that are partly common and partly specific to the entity, thereby respecting the particular characteristics of the local situation and the intended outcomes.

The management of financial structures

55. Universal law and proper law

The temporal goods of the institutes of consecrated life and the societies of apostolic life are seen as ecclesiastical goods that are governed by the provisions of Book V *The Temporal Goods of the Church*, unless expressly directed elsewhere (cf. can. 635 § 1).

The administration of temporal goods, likewise as guided by Book V of the Code of Canon Law, is governed by cann. 634-640 for religious institutes, by can. 718 for the secular institutes, and by can. 741 for societies of apostolic life.

Every institute of consecrated life and society of apostolic life establishes suitable norms regarding the use and administration of goods (cf. can. 635).

56. Roman Pontiff

« The Roman Pontiff, by virtue of the primacy of government, is the supreme administrator and dispenser of all ecclesiastical goods » (can. 1273) and has jurisdiction over them, which is proper to him as the supreme authority of the Church. This power of intervention finds its foundation not in the ownership of ecclesiastical goods, but in the function of the Supreme Pontiff to provide for the supreme government of the Church [7].

57. The Congregation for Institutes of Consecrated Life and Societies of Apostolic Life

The Congregation for Institutes of Consecrated Life and Societies of Apostolic Life «deals with everything which, in accordance with the law, belongs to the Holy See concerning the life and work of the institutes and societies, especially the approval of their constitutions, their manner of government and apostolate, their recruitment and training as well as the rights and obligations of members, dispensation from vows and the dismissal of members, and the administration of goods» [8].

For alienations and acts by which the public juridical person could be damaged, permission is required from the Holy See. The Congregation for Institutes of Consecrated Life and Societies of Apostolic Life, in the

[7] Cf. PONTIFICAL COUNCIL OF LEGISLATIVE TEXTS, Nota, *The function of ecclesiastical authority on ecclesiastical goods* (12 February 2004), in *Communications* 36 (2004), 24-32.

[8] JOHN PAUL II, Ap. Const. *Good Shepherd* (28 June 1988), 108 § 1.

cases provided for by law (cf. can. 638 § 3), issues the permission without, however, assuming any economic responsibilities. The permission guarantees that the transaction « *is congruent with the purposes of the ecclesiastical patrimony.* The delegated responsibility of this intervention is based exclusively on the appropriate exercise of the power of the Church. The permission, therefore, is not an *act of patrimonial domination, but rather of administrative authority* aimed at guaranteeing the good use of the assets of public juridical persons in the Church »[9].

It is the Dicastery's practice to be guided by the maximum amount set by the Episcopal Conferences for the individual regions.

58. The General Chapter

In consecrated life, the management of economic affairs is in harmony with the charism, the mission, and the guidance of poverty. Management decisions that ensure these dimensions must provide adequate forms of community life, avoiding the delega-

[9] Cf. PONTIFICAL COUNCIL OF LEGISLATIVE TEXTS, Nota, *The function of ecclesiastical authority on ecclesiastical goods* (12 February 2004), in *Communications* 36 (2004), 24-32.

tion of economic decisions only to a group or to a single person.

It is up to the *General Chapter*, which « has in the institute the supreme authority according to the norms of the constitutions » (can. 631 § 1), to establish the fundamental ways of proceeding in economic-administrative matters and to elaborate a *charismatic plan* of the institute which also provides corresponding directives.

As the result of a process of a common ecclesial discernment of the will of God, the *charismatic plan* is the fruit of a shared vision, the expression of a synodal journey starting from the pre-chapter stage to its completion in the official reception of the chapter documents.

The Superior General with his/her Council makes operative decisions about the assets and the works in a framework of shared reflection and, if at all possible, not out of an emergency mentality.

The General Chapter prepares and approves an *economic procedures manual* or other similar text, which, also in the light of the experience gained over time, promotes a way of proceeding that is, as much as is feasible, in conformity with the institute's charism, its mission, and the guidance of poverty.

The General Chapter establishes the maximum sum for extraordinary administrative acts for the individual provinces.

The institute's own law determines what are extraordinary administrative acts and the procedures necessary for carrying them out (cf. can. 638 § 1 and can. 1281).

59. Superior and his/her Council

In economic-administrative matters, the Superiors makes use of their own council, according to the universal and proper law (cf. cann. 627 and 638 § 1), and the foundational guidelines established by the General Chapter, especially with respect to extraordinary administrative acts.

60. Provincial Chapter and Provincial Superior

The *Provincial Chapter*, in those institutes who have this, in the light of the *charismatic plan* of the institute approved by the General Chapter, draws up the proposed way to proceed concerning the respective permission that is being sought.

According to the norms established by universal and proper law, the provincial superiors, with the consent of their council, submit to the superiors general along with their council the deeds that require their approval.

When critical issues arise, they should communicate them promptly and with the utmost diligence to the Superiors General, who must be informed by virtue of his/her power over the entire institute in accordance with can. 622.

61. Council for Economic Affairs

According to the norm of can. 1280, the proper law for the institute and for the provinces envisions an advisory council, or some similar body, for economic affairs.

The composition of this body can include collaboration with the laity and with those having specific professional skills. The superiors competent to authorize acts of extraordinary administration, in addition to the consent of their Council (cf. can. 627 § 1), must seek the opinion (cf. can. 127 § 2, 2º) of the Council for Economic Affairs.

62. Administrative Procedures Manual

The competent Superior with his/her Council may adopt, if appropriate, an *administrative procedures manual* – especially in the institutes that manage major public works – which provides operational guidelines within the framework of the *charismatic plan* and the *economic procedures manual.*

The *administrative procedures manual* regulates, among other things, the content, the means, and the schedule about which the competent Superiors must be informed. It should include the activities as well about which they must receive the report. This is valid both for the internal functions of the institute as well as for activities of the civil works and institutions connected to it. Finally, it is essential to make sure that those who are responsible for the oversight of an institution's activities regularly inform the competent Superior about the results of their work.

In order to maintain its effective impact, the *administrative procedures manual* should be known within the institute and should be reviewed periodically through a process that also specifies the timing of such reviews.

63. Commissions

The possibility of setting up commissions or working groups on specific legal-economic issues or facts is determined by an institute's own law. It should state the purpose of the commission, how long the commission shall function, and the process for the appointment of its members. Where appropriate, the participation by professionally qualified lay men and women is advisable.

64. Treasurer

The option whether to elect or name a treasurer is left to the proper law of the institute. In both cases, however, the appointment must take into consideration the growing importance of the necessary professional skills appropriate to the nature of individual institutes (cf. can. 587 § 1), the ability to collaborate with others, the appropriate attitudes for the task (cf. can. 636 § 1), and no personal connection to the assets managed.

Analogous to the canonical norms regarding the term of office for Superiors (can. 624 §§ 1 and 2), the proper law should provide guidance for a defined term of office for the treasurer, and an appropriate transition process that includes appropriate training courses and coaching periods.

It is up to the institute's proper law to determine whether the treasurer should also be a council member. It is appropriate that the treasurer participate in those Council meetings of the Superior that address economic matters. This assures the Superior and his/her Council essential input for an informed decision, even if the treasurer may not have the right to vote since not a council member.

The treasurer is an *ex officio* member of the Council for Economic Affairs referred to in § 61.

The proper law should require regular reporting by the treasurer (cf. cann. 636 § 2 and 1284 § 3) according to procedures identified and periodically evaluated by the superior with his/her council.

Effective means of coordination between the general treasurer, the provincial treasurers, and those responsible for the works are recommended.

65. Legal Representative

The institute, as a legal entity, interacts with third parties through the legal representative (cf. can. 118), both in canonical and in civil arenas.

By carrying out acts in the name of and on behalf of the same institute, he/she implements the decisions made by the legitimate Superiors and the competent bodies, according to universal and proper law, and thereby binds the institute to third parties. For this reason, if deemed appropriate, the legal representative, when not a council member, can participate in meetings of the Council of the Superior in which decisions having civil relevance are made

The legal representative acts always and only within the limits of his/her mandate: he/she can perform the acts of ordinary administration. For extraordinary acts of administration, he/she needs authorization from the competent Superior. On the other hand, when he/she acts without a mandate, either against or beyond it, he/she no longer represents the institute.

If the legal representative acts invalidly, the institute has no responsibility. Acts carried out by the legal representative in this manner are ascribed to him/her and it is he/she who must answer for them. If he/she acts unlawfully, the act is ascribed to the institute which must respond to it, but it can take action against its representative (cf. can. 1281 § 3 and can. 639).

Every single authority delegated to the legal representative, should always be made in precise and clearly written statements. The appropriate procedures for the safekeeping of these documents should be included in a clear policy statement.

For the purpose of having appropriate division of responsibilities, it is preferable that the duties of the legal representative be assumed by a person distinct from the superior or the treasurer, unless civil law provides otherwise.

The organizational structures adopted by the institute regarding the area of competence of the legal representative should also be publicly stated, especially when they interact with civil laws. The timely identification of the matters to be decided and who is authorized to represent the institute constitutes the condition for the establishment of institutional relationships with third parties.

66. Collaboration with external professionals

The increasing complexity of economic-administrative situations often makes it necessary to *collaborate with external professionals.* In choosing external professionals, one should seek those who are knowledgeable of the specifics of the institutes and who are experts in the respective arena, avoiding rash recourse to a single professional.

The professional relationship should stipulate the stated objectives of the activity, include a presentation of budget, and be finalized with clearly written contracts and established timeframes.

It is recommended that the achievement of the established objectives should be evaluated. Further, one should ask the same professionals for periodic reports on the progress of the activity.

67. Internal control

As required by its proper law, institutes should establish procedures of *internal control*, which, through a balanced system of prior authorizations, followed by reports and documentation, allow the competent persons – and in particular the Superior with his/her Council – to supervise the activity of the treasurer, the legal representative, and contracted professionals.

All those who legitimately take part in the administration of ecclesiastical goods, are bound to fulfill their duties in the name of the Church, according to the legal norms (cf. can. 1282).

68. Powers

Particular care is required for the *delegation* of management authority. The authorizations should detail the authority given, its limits – even temporal – and the methods of directing. *General powers* of attorney are to be avoided. In fact, assigning unlimited power to a certain individual to act in the name of and on behalf of the institute exposes the institute to a serious risk of improper behavior and is contrary to the need for open communication and transparency.

The administration and management of the patrimony

69. Civil juridical identity

Institutes of consecrated life and societies of apostolic life should obtain, as far as possible, juridical and civil identity in the countries in which they operate.

The assets are not to be titled in the name of natural persons. In exceptional situations and for serious reasons this may be done, but with the permission of the competent superior. The Superior who has granted the permission shall work to ensure that the property is transferred to the institute as soon as possible with a juridical act that has been validated by civil authority.

Where the institute has to assign the assets to an entity other than a natural person, the Superior who has granted the permission should maintain adequate documentation attesting to the actual ownership, in order to avoid the possibility of civil litigation.

70. Ways of purchase

The work of the members – carried out within their own works or in external works according to the ways permitted by their institute's law and with the permission of the competent Superior (cf. can. 671) – constitutes the ordinary form of sustenance.

In accordance with the can. 668 § 3 all that a religious acquires with his/her own skills and hard work or through the efforts of the institute, is received for the institute. What is received as a pension, subsidy, or insurance for any reason, is acquired for the institute, unless the proper law directs otherwise. Unless otherwise indicated, offerings made to the Superiors or to the administrators of any ecclesiastical juridical person, even a private one, are presumed to be made to the same juridical person (cf. can. 1267 § 1).

The institute has the duty to obtain for the members what, according to the Constitutions, is necessary for them to realize the purpose of their vocation (cf. can. 670).

The proper law establishes the procedures for a valid acceptance of donations. One should pay attention to the characteristics and quality of the donor, to the sources from which these donations may be presumed to come, and to the legitimate rights of third parties. One should not accept donations intended to finance initiatives that, in their purposes or in the means to achieve them, do not correspond to the Church's doctrine.

Although recognizing in them a gift of Providence, the institutes should not accept donations with liabilities (cf. can. 1300) without carefully evaluating the lawfulness of the liabilities, the ability to meet their requirements, and the legitimate rights of third parties.

71. Sharing of assets (cf. § 10)

The institute should establish norms for the equitable sharing of the goods within it, in the spirit of common life, following the example of the first Christian communities (cf. *Acts* 4:34-35). In this way, not only the material goods and the fruit of everyone's work will be shared, but also time, gifts, personal abilities are placed at the service of the apostolic purposes and provide generously for the needs of the less well-off communities: a prophetic witness of fraternity in today's world.

72. Stable Patrimony (cf. §§ 38-40)

The proper law should establish whether the assignment of the assets of the institute to the stable patrimony is the competence of the General Chapter or of the Superior General with the consent of his/her Council. Likewise, with regard to the assets of a legitimately established province or house, the proper law should establish whether the assignment is the task of the provincial chapter or of other similar assemblies (cf. can. 632), or of the provincial superior with consent of his/her Council, and whether it is to be confirmed by the Superior General.

The stable patrimony is composed of the immovable and movable goods that guarantee the subsistence of the institute, the provinces, the legitimately erected houses and assure the realization of the mission.

The assignment of individual assets to the stable assets is subject to periodic evaluation.

The legitimate assignment is required by canon law, regardless of the obligations that the stable patrimony may have in the civil order of the various countries.

The criteria for the management of stable assets should be clearly stated. The budget of the institute, of the province, and of the legitimately erected house should provide a detailed report regarding both the patrimonial and the economic components. In an accompanying report regarding the assets there should be an analysis of any changes that have taken place, the current status, and the use of the asset.

73. Purchase of real estate

Institutes should evaluate with great attention the opportunity to purchase real estate, taking into consideration all aspects related to the decision.

The purchase should be executed and regularized only in ways that would comply with local civil and tax provisions, and at the same time adhere to the *charismatic plan.*

The decision-making process should take the following into consideration: the approval of a specific investment plan that would detail the main factors of the purchase, such as its purpose, the size and intended use; compliance with urban technical norms; the possibility of future alienability; the availability of necessary financial resources or the ways in which these, in whole or in part, will be acquired; a stated outline and plan for the repayment of any loans contracted for this purpose; and a careful evaluation of the seller's qualities.

74. New Constructions

The design and construction of new buildings may start where necessary, observing the previously mentioned conditions for purchases, paying particular attention to the analytic phase and the formulation of precise directions for the designers.

The envisioned structure should have the characteristics of moderation and usefulness. It should be easy to manage, requiring a minimum level of maintenance, both structurally and in the operation of the facility. It should be easily transferable to third parties or convertible to different uses should moments of managerial or vocational difficulties arise.

Vigilant care should be given to the articulation and subsequent implementation of adequate procedures for the assignment of duties and obligations, as well as to control whether what has been planned and accomplished conforms to local legislative regulations.

75. Authorizations of the Holy See for the possible recourse to credit

The proper law should establish the procedure for validly purchasing new assets, for the construction and for the renovation of buildings.

The purchase of assets, new constructions and renovations, although acts of extraordinary administration, no matter the amount, do not require, in accordance with can. 638 § 3, the permission from the Congregation for Institutes of Consecrated Life and Societies of Apostolic Life.

Permission is required where the institute of consecrated life or the society of apostolic life would need to resort to credit for financing the operation in an amount that exceeds the maximum sum provided for each individual region. The documentation to be presented for explaining the transaction is the same as in § 88.

76. Lease of buildings

In the case of leasing of owned assets to third parties and, in general, for all contemplated contracts that place the assets at the disposal of third parties, it is important to carefully evaluate the quality of the tenant; to make sure that the intended use of the asset is not different from the mission of the institute or contrary to the specific nature of temporal goods of the Church and that such is not modifiable over time, unless expressly authorized by the lessor; and to make sure the property is compatible with the proposed use.

The obligations should be correctly established, with attention to the specifications of the contract and its clauses. These specifications should provide for and regulate the processes and conditions by and in which the asset must be returned at the end of the relationship. One should reflect on the resulting implications of the lease, considering that the asset will not be available to the institute for the duration of the relationship.

77. Disposal of assets free of charge

For contracts in which the asset is available free of charge, the same principles apply to the lease. One should pay attention to the liabilities and costs that will be borne by the owner and one should consider who has responsibility for any need for renovations or extraordinary maintenance.

78. Authorizations of the Holy See for leases, loans, and other similar contracts

Regarding any leasing, loans, ceding of land rights, giving use, providing housing, establishing the right of usufruct: should the value of the transaction exceed the maximum amount set for the individual regions and the contract has a duration of over six years, one must seek the authorization of the Congregation for Institutes of Consecrated Life and Societies of Apostolic Life.

The request, sent by the Superior General with the consent of his/her Council, must present the reasons for the request, and attach a draft of the contract.

79. Enhancement of real estate assets

Considering the canonical norms on authorizations (cf. can. 638 §§ 3 and 4), so as to avoid potentially unsustainable future costs, the institutes of consecrated life and societies of apostolic life should initiate an in-depth reflection on how to increase the value of the real estate property in a manner consistent with the nature of an ecclesiastical asset, especially when said assets remains totally or partially unused.

80. Alienation of real estate

The sale of real estate should be done in a manner consistent with the *charismatic plan* of the institute (cf. § 58). The proper law should establish the procedure for validly placing an asset up for sale, as well as for the exchange or donation of real estate, respecting both canonical and civil regulations. Implementing procedures that seek, where possible, the collection of multiple offers should be encouraged.

It is recommended that priority be given, especially where the conditions of the institute allow it, to the possibility of transferring the asset to other ecclesial bodies, avoiding, in any case, alienations that would put in jeopardy the common good of the Church.

Before starting negotiations, one should seek prior knowledge of: the market value of the real estate being sold, whether the asset is completely free and available, whether there exist any restrictions, the existence of necessary documentation from an independent and competent source that clearly states the deed of ownership and the conformity of the property with the current planning regulations. The tax implications should be considered.

In the selection of the purchaser one should consider his/her reputation and – in the instance where payments will be made in installments – whether adequate guarantees have been provided, preferably from a banking or insurance entity.

One should specify in writing any assignment to a third party of the authority to represent or to sell, giving particular attention to all the clauses, especially to any condition under which the operation must be subjected and to the amount of the commission that will be due to the intermediary.

Where possible, the assignment of exclusive mandates should be avoided.

When the characteristics of the bidder, the methods envisaged for the realization of the transaction, or the proposed payment methods do not appear coherent with the values of the respective institutes, the proposal should be rejected.

In accordance with the can. 1298, unless it is a matter of minor importance, ecclesiastical goods must not be sold or leased to employees of the institute or their relatives, up to the fourth degree of consanguinity or affinity, without a special authorization given in writing by the competent Superior.

81. Authorization of the Holy See for the sale or donation of properties

If the value of the asset exceeds the maximum sum set for the individual Regions, in accordance with can. 638 § 3, it is necessary to request the authorization of the Congregation for Institutes of Consecrated Life and Societies of Apostolic Life.

All sales exceeding the maximum amount pursuant to can. 638 § 3, are *valid* only with the authorization of the Congregation for Institutes of Consecrated Life and Societies of Apostolic Life, regardless of whether the goods are ascribed or not to the stable patrimony.

The request for authorization should be presented by the Superior General with the consent of his/her Council. The request should express the just cause (cf. can. 1293 § 1) and define the methods in which the proceeds will be used (cf. can. 1294 § 2). A professional assessment, if possible sworn (cf. can. 1293 § 1, 2nd), should be attached. For institutes of pontifical right, the opinion of the ordinary of the place where the property is located, or for the institutes of diocesan right and the monasteries *sui iuris*, the consent of the ordinary of the place where the property is located (cf. can. 615) should be included.

If the object of the alienation is a divisible asset, for the validity of the authorization the request should indicate the parts of the property which have possibly already been alienated (cf. can. 1292 § 3).

The authorization is also necessary for the sale of several items whose total value exceeds the maximum sum (cf. can. 1292 § 2).

These rules apply for the sale of real estate, contracts for the exchange of goods, for donations even when they involve other public legal entities, provided that their value exceeds the maximum sum.

The Congregation for Institutes of Consecrated Life and Societies of Apostolic Life does not authorize sales aimed at subsidizing immediate financial needs without examining the causes and offering clear proposals for overcoming the actual needs.

When the alienations are indispensable to pay debts that the institute has contracted in carrying out its apostolic works, it is necessary that in the dossier a plan for economic-financial rehabilitation be presented.

The Congregation for Institutes of Consecrated Life and Societies of Apostolic Life, in accordance with can. 1293 § 2, may require the inclusion of other precautions to avoid damage to the Church.

For the sale of buildings located in the city of Rome, before issuing the authorization, the Congregation for Institutes of Consecrated Life and Societies of Apostolic Life shall communicate the request to the Secretariat of State and to the Administration of the Patrimony of the Apostolic See, to determine whether they would have possible interest in the property.

For the authorization of the alienation of property located in Malta the norms established by the *Statutum* of 6 July 1988 apply.

For real estate located in the Middle East, competence belongs to the Congregation for the Oriental Churches.

82. Authorization of the Holy See for precious items of artistic or historical value and for votive donations

Permission is required for the alienation of precious items that have artistic or historical value even if the amount does not exceed the maximum sum. Where these assets are subject to regulations, the requirements laid down by the relevant civil laws are followed.

The disposal of votive donations made to the Church are subject to the same discipline. It is absolutely illegal to sell sacred relics (cf. can. 1190 § 1).

The sacred items, if they belong to a public ecclesiastical juridical person, can be acquired only by another public ecclesiastical juridical person (cf. can. 1269).

83. Alienations without the required permission

In accordance with the can. 1296, when ecclesiastical goods were disposed of without respect for canonical norms, and the alienation proves to be civilly valid, the competent superior will have to decide whether to take appropriate actions to claim the rights of the Church.

In accordance with the can. 1377, the one who alienates ecclesiastical goods without the proper authorization will receive the punishment due.

84. Financial investments

In the use and management of financial assets not immediately required for the institute's activities (so-called *financial investments*), there should be knowledge of the technical complexity of market procedures. Appropriate and prudent criteria should be followed in the choices and selection of financial products offered. One should investigate the legality of the procedure and the ethical nature of the investment, giving particular attention to the aims of the institute and to the health and retirement needs of its members.

Given the technical complexity of the decisions in such matters, the directives offered above regarding the economic choices and the selection of the professionals are valid.

85. Works (cf. § 34)

It is advisable to evaluate whether works of considerable size should be distinct from the institute of consecrated life or from the society of apostolic life, according to what is or will be established by universal and proper law. The solutions may be determined in various ways according to the specific circumstances. One should ensure the fidelity of the work to the charism of the institute and its compliance with established modes of relations between the State and the Church.

Particular attention should be given to those works that are evangelically significant but characterized, due to the changing context and general conditions, by a structural economic vulnerability. The institutes should seek solutions that prevent negative economic developments that could compromise the goals that correspond to the mission of the Church (cf. can. 114 § 1).

There are other works in which there will always be inherent economic vulnerability. The respective institute should realistically assess whether there are resources available appropriate to the task, making the necessary decisions in a timely manner.

In the presence of economic or managerial difficulties, it is opportune to investigate the possibility of implementing ways of collaborating with other institutes or of transforming the work itself in such a way that it continues, albeit in different ways, as a work of the Church.

Prudence would suggest making decisions as soon as possible, so as to avoid the convergence of negative economic trends or, even, the necessity to proceed with the closure of the work.

In the event that the management has become excessively complex or burdensome, one could designate assets that ascribe ownership of the assets and control of the work to be that of the institute, while entrusting the operational management to third parties, in a manner respectful of the charism and supportive of the mission of the institute.

86. Authorizations of the Holy See for the disposal of works

For the sale of works when the value exceeds the maximum sum set for each Region, it is necessary to obtain permission from the Congregation for Institutes of Consecrated Life and Societies of Apostolic Life.

The procedure is the same as is established for the sale of real estate (cf. § 81).

For the disposal or reorganization of health or social-health works in the Italian territory, the Congregation for Institutes of Consecrated Life and Societies of Apostolic Life transmits the request to the *Pontifical Commission for the Activities of Public Juridical*

Persons of the Church in the Healthcare Sector, from which eventual authorization will be received.

87. Incurring Debt

The proper law should establish the procedures for validly contracting mortgages, debts, securities.

The competent Superiors, according to the norm of can. 639 § 5, should refrain from approving the contracting of a debt, unless it is ascertained that the interest on the debt can be covered by ordinary income, and that the entire capital can be repaid within a not too extended period of time given a reasonable amortization.

Adherence to the essential elements of this requirement occurs when: the activity is different from the nature of the work itself, requires the adoption and implementation of appropriate organizational structures, effective accounting procedures and resources, effective management reporting, adequate supervisory committees, and internal control structures.

Having received a proposal to incur debt, it will be the task of the Superior with his/her Council to assess whether the proposal is adequately studied and whether all the necessary elements needed for an informed decision are available. He/She will have to consider the reasonableness of the assumptions on which the prospects for income are based, considering the impact of any pre-existing debt as well.

When it is necessary to issue a guarantee for the financing, careful consideration should be given to whether the amount is appropriate, to consideration of the terms of its release, and the possible implications of making such a guarantee. The evaluation process will have to be particularly thorough when the guarantee is required by a legally distinct entity, whether it be a contracted or partnership relationship.

The superior with his/her Council should require periodic examination of the overall financial situation of the entity seeking to incur debt, reviewing its actual sustainability. When its size, its composition, its foreseeable evolution highlight a critical condition, he/she should evaluate the situation and take timely action.

When pertinent, any risks related to possible currency fluctuations should be taken into consideration.

In accordance with the can. 639 § 1, the juridical person who has contracted debts and charges, even with the permission of the Superiors, is obliged to answer for it on his/her own. If a religious with permission from the Superior has contracted debts and charges to his/her own assets, he/she must personally answer it; if instead by mandate of the superior he/she has conducted the institute's business, it is the institute that is responsible for it (cf. can. 639 § 2). If the religious contracts debts without any permission from the superior, it will be he/she, and not the juridical person, who is responsible (cf. can. 639 § 3).

88. Authorization of the Holy See for financing

When the amount of the financial transaction exceeds the maximum amount set for the individual Regions, for the validity of the act, the authorization of the Congregation for Institutes of Consecrated Life and Societies of Apostolic Life is required.

The Superior General shall forward the request after having obtained the consent of his/her Council, indicating the reasons, presenting the overall debt situation of the institute, and the amortization plan.

If the request for financing is because of a crisis in the works, the Congregation for Institutes of Consecrated Life and Societies of Apostolic Life does not grant authorization unless it has studied in detail the reasons that have generated the economic difficulties.

In the case of significant amounts without financial budgetary documentation, the Dicastery may not grant authorizations to requests for financing.

89. Associated civil entities

Given the specific modes of relationship between the State and the Church in individual countries and the concrete choices of organization of each institute, it often happens that *civil entities are frequently linked to the canonical juridical person.*

The proper law should establish the procedures for constituting civil entities connected to the institute and for transferring assets to them.

Although they are legally distinct entities, the connection of these institutions to the institutes justifies particular attention as to how they are constituted and managed. The activity of these institutions, in fact, can put at risk the good reputation of the institute and give rise, if the applicable civil laws provide for it, to the institute having a responsibility for debts of the associated institution.

Acknowledging canonical legislation, the ways of managing associated civil entities should be in conformity with the charism of institutes of consecrated life and societies of apostolic life. To this end, the methods that can be used are many, for example: the provision in the statutes of associated civil entities stating purposes similar to those of institutes of consecrated life and societies of apostolic life; the attribution to the governing bodies of the institutes and companies the power to appoint the managers and to approve the extraordinary administrative acts of the associated civil entities; the provision of obligatory reports to institutes by the heads of associated civil entities; the insertion in the statutes of such institutions of a clause that, in the case of dissolution, indicates that the residual patrimony returns to the institute of consecrated life or to the society of apostolic life, to another connected civil institution or to another institute or society with similar characteristics. In no case may recourse to civil entities be used in any manner to circumvent the canonical controls.

90. Authorization of the Holy See for transfer of assets to civil entities

When the value of the good to be transferred to the civil entity, even if connected to the institute, exceeds the maximum sum established for each Region, the permission of the Congregation for Institutes of Consecrated Life and Societies of Apostolic Life is required. For directions on procedures to be followed, refer to what has been said for buildings, in § 81 of this document and for works in § 86.

91. The duty to give an account
   (cf. §§ 41-43)

The general duty to give an account, as provided for by canonical norms (cf. can. 636 § 2), promotes orderly management and ensures the sustainability of institutes of consecrated life and societies of apostolic life.

Every directive regarding reporting and financial statements is to be followed according to the principle of *proportionality*. For this reason, it takes into consideration, first of all, the addressee, with its particular nature, its dimensions, its specific activity, and the historical and social environment in which it operates.

The duty to report, therefore, requires the keeping of *accounting records* proportionate to the size and organizational characteristics of individual institutes. These reports in any case provide the identification, with the aid of information systems, of the patrimonial, economic, and financial data relative to the communities and works. In this perspective, the *financial statements* become a helpful tool for making informed choices through increased transparency in management and, at the same time, give credibility to the institute in its civil community.

For institutions spread through several countries, it is advisable to adopt adequate accounting methods to allow comparison and, where appropriate, aggregation of data.

For the works, it is necessary to keep separate accounts and, in the case of works of considerable size, it is strongly recommended to submit the financial statements for *external auditing*. With works having particular social value, the preparation of an *outcomes report* can contribute to a greater awareness of the results of its activities, and to transparency in institutional relations and fundraising.

With reference to the works, in order to effectively use the available resources, it is advisable: to adopt adequate tools to define the medium-long term objectives (i.e. *strategic planning*); to implement economic-financial planning (i.e. *budgeting*); to have ongoing evaluation to verify if the envisioned objectives are attained (i.e. *management control*);

and to identify responsible personnel and implementation procedures proportional to the size and specific nature of the activities.

92. The application of civil laws

In any case, respect for civil laws is necessary. Particular attention should be paid to the treatment of workers. It is important to make sure to observe carefully the laws relating to work and social life, according to the principles of the social doctrine of the Church. The employees should be paid justly and honestly, so that they are able to adequately provide for their own needs and those of their families (cf. can. 1286).

Attention should also be given to the obligations to creditors, tax and social security charges, and the prevention of criminal acts.

93. Record keeping (cf. § 44)

In accordance with can. 1283 and 1284, each institute should keep appropriate economic and administrative files for the purposes of an efficient administration and proper accounting of data. One should diligently attend to the compilation and the constant updating of the inventory of assets and inventory, as well as to the careful cataloging and preservation of accounting records and insurance policies.

Relationships in the Church

94. Relations with the local Church
(cf. §§ 28-30)

The Major Superiors should seek to cooperate with the Church in the projects of the institute as well in their management. In this way, before the closure of a community or of a work – for which the prior consultation of the diocesan bishop (cf. cann. 612 and 678 § 3) is requested – the possibility of concrete alternative solutions can be discussed.

The institutes of pontifical right, before sending the request for authorization for the alienation of buildings and the suppression of works to the Congregation for Institutes of Consecrated Life and Societies of Apostolic Life, should ask for the written opinion of the ordinary of the place where the property is located.

In accordance with the can. 638 § 4, the institutes of diocesan right and the monasteries *sui iuris* (cf. can. 615), should request, for the same matters, the written consent of the local ordinary.

The monasteries *sui iuris*, referred to in can. 615, should make an annual report to the local ordinary regarding their administration. The latter has the right to examine the state of the economic affairs of a religious house of diocesan right (cf. can. 637).

Many consecrated women dedicate themselves, even full-time, to diocesan pastoral care or to offices and duties related to it. This *feminine ministry* offers its own experience and expertise, even a recognized professionalism. It is up to the Major Superiors, in accord to what is prescribed in can. 681 § 2, to determine through agreements with the respective local Churches exactly what constitutes the service of the consecrated person and the economic aspects of that same service.

95. Collaboration among institutes
(cf. §§ 31-33)

In order to foster collaboration among institutes, periodic meetings between the general treasurers are to be fostered, above all when there is an affinity of charisms and works. Shared moments of formation and study are encouraged with teachers and experts of the fields pertaining to the operations of the institutes. Forms of collaboration may be created for the organization and management of the necessary administrative and accounting services, thereby developing concrete forms of solidarity. There could also be the creation of funds for the benefit of institutes in conditions of greater difficulty.

The Conferences of the Major Superiors, in addition to fostering collaboration and dialogue, could assist in explaining the socio-political and legislative changes taking place in order to encourage more effective decisions by individual institutes. They could foresee, where possible, commissions consisting of consecrated men and women as well as of laity, all experts in economic matters, to which institutes could turn to compare their experiences, and – especially when they are of modest size and resources – to seek advice, support, and good practices.

96. Relations with the Congregation for Institutes of Consecrated Life and Societies of Apostolic Life

Occasional conferences, meetings in the Dicastery, together with the *Periodic Report on the State and Life of the Institutes of Consecrated Life and Societies of Apostolic Life* (cf. can. 592 § 1), are effective means for responding to the need for mutual understanding, which arises out of the required interaction of institutes of consecrated life and societies of apostolic life with the Holy See.

In the *periodic report,* institutes should give particular attention to the information required by this Congregation [10] with respect to the economic condition of the institutes of consecrated life and societies of apostolic life and their long-range plans, so as to have an adequate knowledge base. It is also helpful for diplomatic dialogue with the states.

A more developed understanding of the discipline of permissions (cf. can. 638 § 3) is desirable, especially in the case of alienations or other acts that may cause detriment to the financial situation of the institute. In particular, more information is needed when the acts relate to the social security needs and the livelihood of the members of the institute, or when they become part of a strategic decision on the maintenance, on the disposal of the works, or in a bankruptcy procedure for the management of relations with creditors.

The request for authorization becomes an opportunity for a frank dialogue that, without jeopardizing the legitimate autonomy of the

[10] CONGREGATION FOR INSTITUTES OF CONSECRATED LIFE AND SOCIETIES OF APOSTOLIC LIFE, *Guidelines for the drafting of the periodic report on the state and life of Institutes of Consecrated Life and Societies of Apostolic Life* (cf. CIC can. 592 §1), Attached to Prot. n. SpR 640/2008.

institutes, safeguards a respect for the ecclesiastical nature of the goods and the community dynamics proper to the Church.

In the presence of significant economic problems, this Dicastery can intervene directly in the life of institutes of consecrated life and societies of apostolic life through Apostolic Visitors and Pontifical Commissioners. These occasions should be adopted as a signs of the solicitude of the Holy See to which the task of care, promotion, and oversight of the institutes is entrusted.

97. Formation to the economic dimension (cf. §§ 18-19)

It is the specific task of the Superiors to begin or to strengthen the *economic dimension* of formation programs both in a broad sense with regard to the Social Doctrine of the Church, and specifically with attention to economic-administrative challenges.

Particular significance, in view of the economic dimension of formation, should be given to budgets. These must not be understood solely in their indispensable technical aspects, but also should be understood as means to grow in common life, in co-responsibility, and in the ability to plan the life and development of the works in a manner coherent with the mission and the general and/or provincial *charismatic plan.*

Respecting the legitimate autonomy of the institutes – especially given the complexities of management – appropriate forms of ongoing formation must be pursued, in conjunction with Catholic universities or other specialized institutions that combine technical competence with awareness of the issues specific to consecrated life.

Careful attention should be given to the *training of treasurers* and other members of the institute with positions of responsibility in economic matters.

Superiors should obtain all the necessary pieces of information to evaluate the issues submitted for their attention.

One should not neglect the *formation of the laity* called to collaborate with the institutes, to ensure that their behaviour conforms to the charism and serves the mission. In addition to proposals aimed at safeguarding and improving the necessary professional competence one should offer to the lay staff employed by the institute access to a formation program that is global, focused, integrated, and ongoing.

CONCLUSION

98. Consecrated persons are called to be *good stewards of the varied forms of God's grace* (*1 Pt.* 4:10), *prudent and faithful* administrators (*Lk.* 12:42), with the task of diligently taking care of what has been entrusted to them.

« We have received talents from God, *according to ability of each* (*Mt.* 25:15). Before all else, let us realize this: we do have talents; in God's eyes, we are "talented". Consequently, no one can think that he or she is useless, so poor as to be incapable of giving something to others. We are chosen and blessed by God, who wants to fill us with His gifts, more than any father or mother does with their own children. And God, in whose eyes no child can be neglected, entrusts to each of us a mission » [1].

The primacy belongs to the gift of the invitation to be « a living memorial of Jesus' way of living and acting as the Incarnate Word in relation to the Father and in relation to the brethren » [2].

---

[1] FRANCIS, *Homily* on the occasion of the First World Day of the Poor, Rome (19 November 2017).

[2] JOHN PAUL II, Post Synod Ap. Ex. *Consecrated Life* (25 March 1996), 22.

The world needs more and more people who by the grace of God give themselves totally, « men and women capable of accepting the abnegation of poverty, and of being attracted by simplicity and humility; it is that of those who love peace, who are free from compromise and set on complete self-denial of those who are at the same time free and obedient, spontaneous and tenacious, meek and strong in the certainty of the Faith »[3].

Consecrated men and women, embracing the evangelical counsel of poverty, are the *living memory* of the poor Christ for the poor. While they testify by their life to having found the precious pearl (*Mt.* 13:45-46), they choose to share the lot of the poor, because « evangelical poverty is a value in itself, since it recalls the first of the Beatitudes in the imitation of the poor Christ »[4].

99. The poor urge us to make concrete choices, to assume, even in outward signs, a life that is consistently simple and moderate. Called to follow the poor Christ, new forms will be sought to express the joy of the Gospel

[3] PAUL VI, Ap. Ex. *Evangelica testificatio* (29 June 1971), 31.

[4] JOHN PAUL II, Post Synod Ap. Ex. *Consecrated Life* (25 March 1996), 90.

through a clearer testimony of poverty that is as personal as it is communal.

Even today, the Lord multiplies for us the five loaves and the two fishes (*Jn.* 6:9), beginning from the gifts that so many fellow Christians place in our hands to feed those in need. To live in a manner in which one is touched by Providence means knowing how to welcome what God sends for our life and open our hands to give it back to the poor.

The goods and the works are entrusted to us as a gift of a providential God for accomplishing the mission. Their correct stewardship, for which some ways of proceeding have been offered, allows us to live the evangelical counsel of poverty and to be faithful to the charisms given to the Founders and Foundresses, at the service of the Church's mission.

Pope Francis often teaches insistently in his addresses that one should speak less of poverty and more of the poor. The poor, then, are the principle that includes the one and the many, which guides the mission. In this straining towards the Kingdom, the Church realizes herself and in her consecrated life becomes fruitful.

« Let us never forget that, for Christ's disciples, poverty is above all a *call to follow Jesus in his own poverty*. It means walking behind Him and beside Him, a journey that leads to the beatitude of the Kingdom of heaven (cf. *Mt.* 5:3, *Lk.* 6:20). Poverty means having a humble heart that accepts our creaturely limitations and sinfulness and thus enables us to overcome the temptation to feel omnipotent and immortal. Poverty is an interior attitude that avoids looking upon money, career, and luxury as our goal in life and the condition for our happiness. Poverty instead creates the conditions for freely shouldering our personal and social responsibilities, despite our limitations, with trust in God's closeness and the support of His grace. Poverty, understood in this way, is the yardstick that allows us to judge how best to use material goods and to build relationships that are neither selfish nor possessive » [5].

Approved by the Holy Father
in an audience on December 12, 2017

Vatican City, January 6, 2018
Solemnity of the Epiphany of the Lord

João Braz Card. de Aviz
Prefect

✠ José Rodríguez Carballo, O.F.M.
Archbishop Secretary

---

[5] FRANCIS, *Message on the occasion of the First World Day of the Poor*, Rome (13 June 2017), 4.

INDEX

D PRINT – ROMA